How To Multiply Your Baby's Intelligence

MORE GENTLE REVOLUTION

other works in the gentle revolution series

How to Teach Your Baby Math
How to Teach Your Baby to Read
How to Give Your Baby Encyclopedic
    Knowledge
How to Teach Your Baby to Be Physically
    Superb
What to Do About Your Brain-Injured Child

children's books

Enough, Inigo, Enough
Noses Is Not Toes
The Moose Book
The Wrong Cockatiel
Nanki Goes to Nova Scotia

How To Multiply Your Baby's Intelligence

MORE GENTLE REVOLUTION

Glenn Doman
Janet Doman

Avery Publishing Group

Garden City Park, New York

Photographer: Stan Schnier, NYC
Printer: Paragon Press, Honesdale, PA

Cataloging in Publication Data

Doman, Glenn J.
   How to multiply your baby's intelligence : more gentle revolution
/ by Glenn Doman, Janet Doman.
   p. cm. — (The gentle revolution series)
   Includes index.
   ISBN 0-89529-601-2 (hard)
   ISBN 0-89529-600-4 (pbk.)

   1. Children—Intelligence levels. 2. Cognition in children. 3.
Child rearing. I. Doman, Janet. II. Title. III. Series.

BF432.C48D66 1994   649'.68
                                               QBI93-21712

Printed in the United States of America

10   9   8

contents

1
the Gentle Revolution

The Gentle Revolution began quietly, ever so quietly, more than a quarter of a century ago. It was and is the most gentle of all revolutions. It is possibly the most important of revolutions and surely the most glorious.

Consider first the objective of the Gentle Revolution: to give all parents the knowledge required to make highly intelligent, extremely capable and delightful children, and by so doing to make a highly humane, sane and decent world.

Consider next the revolutionaries—as unlikely

a bunch as can be imagined. There are three groups of them.

First there are the newborn babies of the world, who have always been there with their vast, almost undreamed-of potential.

Second there are the mothers and fathers who have always had their dreams as to what their babies might become. Who could have believed that their wildest dreams might actually fall short of the real potential?

Finally there is the staff of the Institutes for the Achievement of Human Potential, who since 1940 have come to recognize the stunning truth about children, truth over which they have tripped time and time again during the many years they have searched for it.

Babies, mothers, staff—an unlikely bunch to bring about the most important revolution in history.

And what an unlikely revolution.

Who ever heard of a revolution in which there is no death, no pain, no torture, no torment, no bloodshed, no hatred, no starvation, no destruction? Who ever heard of a *gentle* revolution?

In this most gentle of revolutions there are two foes. The first are those most implacable of enemies, The Ancient Myths, and the second is that most formidable foe, The Way Things Are.

It is not necessary that old traditions be destroyed but only that long-held false beliefs wither away unmourned. It is not necessary that what is of value today be smashed to bits but only that those things which are presently destructive dissolve as a product of disuse.

Who would mourn the demise of ignorance, incompetence, illiteracy, unhappiness and poverty?

Would not the elimination of such ancient foes bring about a gentler world with less need for violence, killing, hatred and war—or perhaps no need at all?

What discoveries could possibly have led to such lovely dreams?

What happened more than a quarter of a century ago?

Our first realization was that it is possible to teach babies to read. As unlikely as that sounded it is not only true but it is even true that it is easier to teach a one-year-old to read than it is to teach a seven-year-old. Much easier.

By 1964 we had written a book for mothers called *How to Teach Your Baby to Read.* That book was an instant success and the Gentle Revolution began. Scores of mothers wrote almost immediately to tell of their joy in reading the book and their success in teaching their children.

Then hundreds wrote to tell what had happened to their children after they had learned to read. Thousands of mothers bought the book and taught their babies to read.

The book was published in British and Australian editions and in Afrikaans, Dutch, Finnish, French, German, Greek, Hebrew, Indonesian, Italian, Japanese, Norwegian, Malay, Portuguese, Spanish and Swedish.

Tens of thousands of mothers wrote to tell us of what had happened. What those mothers reported with delight and pride was that

1. Their babies had easily learned to read;
2. Their babies had loved learning;
3. Mother and baby had increased the degree of love between them (which they reported with much pleasure but no surprise);
4. The amount of respect of mother for child and child for mother had grown by leaps and bounds (this they reported with much joy and a good deal of surprise);
5. As their children's ability to read grew, their love of learning grew and so did their abilities in many things.

Today that book is in eighteen languages and more than two million mothers have bought *How to Teach Your Baby to Read* in hardback in English.

Every day letters arrive from mothers, as they have since 1964. Those letters are paeans, and the song of joy and praise they sing is of the vast potential of their babies at the first instants of its realization.

These mothers tell us of the confirmation of their intuitive feelings about their babies' innate abilities and of their own absolute determination that their children should have every opportunity to be all they are capable of being.

As we go around the world and to every continent we get to talk to thousands of mothers individually and in groups. In the most sophisticated societies and in the simplest ones we ask this question:

"Would every mother in the group who thinks her child is doing as well as he ought to be doing, please put up her hand."

It's always the same. Nobody moves.

Perhaps they are just bashful so we reverse the question to see if that's what it is:

"Will every mother in the room who thinks her child is not doing as well as he could be doing, please put up her hand."

Now every hand in the room goes up.

Everybody in the world knows that something is wrong in the world of children—but nobody does anything about it.

Perhaps nobody does anything about it because, like the weather, nobody knows precisely what to do.

After almost a half a century of work with mothers and children which has been at once joyous and painstaking, and a long series of the most fortuitous accidents, we have learned what's right and what we think should be done about it. We have learned how things might be—how things could be—No! How things should be, with the kids of the world.

For some time now it has been clear to us that mothers have been absolutely right in their certainty that their kids are not doing as well as they should be.

It has, for some time, been clear to us why mothers and fathers have been right in believing that their kids have a right to a great deal more out of life than they are getting.

If parents have been in any way wrong about all of this, it has been in not knowing how right they've been.

We now know beyond any shadow of a doubt that

1. Children *want* to multiply their intelligence;
2. Children *can* multiply their intelligence;
3. Children *are* multiplying their intelligence;

4. Children *should* multiply their intelligence;
5. It is easy to teach mothers how to multiply their children's intelligence.

More importantly, since the 1960s we've actually been teaching mothers to raise their children's intelligence by leaps and bounds and they've been doing it, although, decades ago, neither they nor we saw it in exactly that light.

Since the early 1970s we and our parents have not only been raising children's intelligence by remarkable amounts but we have known precisely what we've been up to.

We are pragmatic people who are much more influenced by the facts than by anyone's theories, including our own.

It has all worked out beautifully, putting aside a number of reasonably painful knocks along the way, with more joyful, angry, happy, miserable, hilarious, agonizing, rewarding, extremely frustrating, mind boggling, uplifting, delightful sessions at 3:00 a.m. than any one of us can remember.

Our days are still intoxicating and provocative beyond measure and none of us would trade our lives for any other.

But in our very busy Eden there is one large problem; one question we have not answered to our own satisfaction; one final pull on our collective conscience.

Almost everyone whom we have come to know has asked us the question that we ask ourselves constantly.

"And is it not true that if a group of people has gained special and perhaps vital knowledge of the babies of the world, whether purposely or by accident, those people, whether they like it or not, have, in fact, a special obligation to all the children of the world?"

It is obvious that the answer to that question is, "Yes, we do have a special obligation to all the children of the world."

We have an obligation to every child in the world to tell his mother and father what we have learned so that they may decide what, if anything, they would like to do about it.

If the future of every tiny kid in the world has to be decided by somebody else (and clearly it does) then that somebody else must be his parents.

We would fight for a mother's or father's right to do or not to do the things this book proposes.

We have a duty to tell every mother and father alive what we have learned.

It is easy and joyful to teach a twelve-month-old to read.

It is easy and joyful to teach a twelve-month-old to do math (better than I can).

It is easy and joyful to teach a twelve-month-old to understand, and to read, a foreign language (or two or three languages, if you like).

It is easy and joyful to teach a twenty-eight-month-old how to write (not write words—write stories and plays).

It is easy and joyful to teach a newborn infant how to swim (even if you can't).

It is easy and joyful to teach an eighteen-month-old how to do gymnastics (or ballet or how to fall down the stairs without hurting himself).

It is easy and joyful to teach an eighteen-month-old how to play the violin, or the piano, or whatever.

It is easy and joyful to teach an eighteen-month-old about birds, flowers, trees, insects, reptiles, sea shells, mammals, fishes, their names, identification, scientific classifications, or whatever else about them you wish to teach.

It is easy and joyful to teach an eighteen-month-old about presidents, kings, flags, continents, countries, states.

It is easy and joyful to teach an eighteen-month-old how to draw or paint or to—well, to teach him to do anything which you can present to him in an honest and factual way.

When you teach a tiny child even one of these things his intelligence rises.

When you teach a tiny child several of these things his intelligence rises sharply.

When you teach all these things to a tiny child with joy and love and respect, his intelligence is *multiplied.*

And best of all, when parents who truly love and respect their babies give them the gift of knowledge and ability children are happier, kinder and more caring than children who have not been given these opportunities.

Children who are taught with love and respect do not become nasty little monsters. How could knowledge and truth given as a joyful gift create nastiness?

They cannot and they do not.

If they did, then the staff of the Institutes, who love and respect children, would quietly forget all the knowledge to which they have fallen heir.

However the opposite is the case—*knowledge does lead to good.*

Children who are the most competent are the most self-sufficient. They have the least reason to whine and the most reason to smile.

Children who are the brightest have the least reason to demand help.

Children who have the most ability have the

least need to hit other children.

Children who have the most ability have the least reason to cry and the greatest reason to do things.

In short, the children who are truly bright, knowledgeable and capable are the nicest children and the most understanding of others. They are full of the characteristics for which we love children.

It is the least competent, incapable, insensitive, unknowing child who whines, cries, complains and hits.

In short, it is with children just about the way it is with adults.

We recognize that we do, in fact, have a duty to tell all mothers and fathers what we have learned so that they may consider it.

We have a duty to tell all mothers that they are, and have always been—the best teachers the world has ever seen.

This book, like *How to Teach Your Baby to Read, How To Teach Your Baby Math* and the other books in the Gentle Revolution Series, is our way of meeting that delightful obligation.

The objective of the Gentle Revolution is to give every child alive, through his parents, his chance to be excellent.

And we, together, are the revolutionists.

If this be treason, make the most of it.

It is the hope of the staff of the Institutes that you and your baby have as much joy, pleasure, excitement, discovery and exultation in using this knowledge as we've had in stumbling into it over all the years of exploration.

A Note To Parents

There are no chauvinists at the Institutes, either male or female. We love and respect mothers and fathers, baby boys and baby girls. To solve the maddening problems of referring to all human beings as "grown-up male persons" or "tiny female persons" we have decided to refer to all parents as mothers and to all children as boys.

Seems fair.

2
the nature of myths

When we human beings get a myth into our minds, it is almost impossible to get it out—even when all the seeable, hearable, measurable facts stand in direct opposition to the myth; even when the truth is a great deal better, more important, easier and substantially more delightful than the myth.

Although humans had stood on hilltops for tens of thousands of years and looked at the ocean horizon curve, we remained persuaded that the earth was flat until a mere five hundred years ago. Some are still persuaded that it is flat.

Almost all myths severely denigrate the truth.

No myths denigrate the truth more severely than those which deal with mothers, babies and geniuses.

Mothers, babies and geniuses have a bad press.

Sometime we must find out why our myths should downgrade mothers, babies and geniuses.

If we ever have time to discover why this should be so we may find out that some people in our society feel threatened by mothers, babies and geniuses. Perhaps we'll find that there are those who, for some reason, feel a little inferior to them.

In some cases our lives are dominated, and diminished, by the myths with which we live.

Almost all myths are negative and were originally invented to harm or destroy some group of people.

How is it possible for us to stoutly, and even devoutly, hold hundreds, or even thousands, of unshakable beliefs when the evidence that they are patently untrue is all around us on a daily or even hourly basis?

So very much of what I hear does not come from the sound to my ear to my brain, as physiologically it must, if I am to understand what I hear.

Instead I am a victim of my own myths and prejudices and so I hear precisely what I *wish* to hear.

Thus I decide in advance what you are going to say, and regardless of what you say, I hear exactly what I *thought* I was going to hear (in fact what I *wanted* to hear).

What you said did not come from your mouth to my ear to my brain as physiology dictates in lesser creatures.

Because I am human, and cursed by the myths that influence me, I am able to subvert even physiological function and thus what you said came from *my* brain to my ear to my brain and you have said precisely what I knew you were going to say in the first place.

I also do not see what is before me, but instead, what I *thought* I was going to see.

May I give you a single, clear example?

I would like to draw a face.

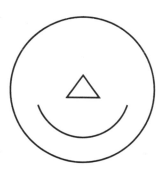

So far, complete with ears, nose and mouth it could be any kind of face.

Now I would like to draw two additional lines, and with two simple lines it will become a very particular kind of face.

What kind of face is it now?

With the simple addition of two short straight lines, I have made it a Japanese face. This is because (as everyone knows) Japanese have slanted eyes.

Close your eyes and imagine a typical Japanese face.

Do you see those slanted eyes? Indeed are not the slanted eyes the single most characteristic feature in a Japanese face?

That is to say, they are—unless you happen to be Japanese.

The fact is that Japanese do *not* have slanted

eyes. In fact, Japanese eyes are as flat as a pancake.

I learned this unheard-of fact one day while having lunch with a close Japanese friend in Tokyo.

I was holding forth quite earnestly on this very subject and wondering aloud how it was possible to look at reality and to see its exact opposite.

"Exactly," said my Japanese friend, "And a perfect example is the western belief that the Japanese have slanted eyes."

"Oh, but the Japanese do have slanted eyes," said I looking him squarely in his flat-as-a-billiard-table Japanese eyes.

Before my eyes I watched his slanted eyes actually become flat.

"But your eyes are flat," I said accusingly as if he were, in fact, not actually Japanese.

I looked around the crowded restaurant only to find that every Japanese diner in the place had eyes which were extraordinarily flat. My instantaneous question to myself was, how in the world had they managed to get every Japanese alive with un-Japanese eyes into a single restaurant?

I felt extremely uncomfortable.

I have never minded exploding everybody else's myths in a gentle and good natured way but I thought it rather rude of my ordinarily very polite Japanese friend to bring the fact that Japanese eyes are indeed flat to my attention so forcefully.

Take a hard look at the next Japanese friend you meet and pay special attention to how very parallel to the ground his eyes are.

But until you actually have an opportunity to examine a pair of Japanese eyes up close why don't you try an experiment right at this moment?

Try closing your eyes again, and again picture in your mind a Japanese face. See those slanted eyes?

Myths die very hard in the most open minded of us, it is almost impossible to get rid of them in most of us and it is impossible to substitute reality in a good many of us.

In eyes, as in earth, we humans have difficulty differentiating flat from curved or slanted.

This book has as its primary objective differentiating long-held myths from facts, especially as they relate to little kids, parents in general and mothers in particular, intelligence, the human brain and geniuses.

About kids, mothers, intelligence, the brain and geniuses there are unending myths. That these myths are patently absurd has completely failed to diminish their almost universal acceptance—most especially on the part of professional people who should know better.

So absurd and ridiculous are these myths that they would be high humor were not the result of them so tragic.

3

the genesis of genius

We, of all people, should have known. We, the staff of the Institutes for the Achievement of Human Potential, should have known a whole lot better and a whole lot sooner.

We should have known before anybody else, not because we're smarter than anybody else, but because living with so many different kinds of little children and their parents, twenty-four hours a day for forty years or longer as we have, caused us to trip over the truth so much more often than anybody else.

We should have known a long time ago that every human infant has within her or him the seeds of genius.

We should have known, in time long past, that

1. We are members of that group called *Homo sapiens,* and because we are members of this group we each inherit the genes that provide us with the unique human cortex;
2. We are born into an environment which either provides stimulation or it does not;
3. Every time a baby is born, the potential for genius is born again with that baby.

He arrives with the great genetic gift of the human cortex. The only question is what kind of environment will we provide for that human cortex to grow and develop?

Genius is available to every human infant. We should have known this in our bellies, by our experience; and in our minds, by our knowledge. The genesis of genius lies, not alone in our ancient common ancestral genes, but as a seed that may be brought to full fruit in each tiny human infant.

We should have known full well, years ago, that genius is not a gift endowed on a few by a God who, through wishing some very small number of his children to be vastly superior, wished the vast majority of his children to be inferior.

Even less is genius a blind accident occurring once in a hundred, a thousand, or a million years without rhyme or reason.

We should have known—twenty, twenty-five, perhaps fifty years ago—that what we call genius, a uniquely human capacity of the uniquely human cortex, is no gift at all.

Instead it is a human birthright common to all, out of which we have been cheated by our lack of knowledge. It is a superb opportunity which has been stolen from a family of creatures who have genius as their birthright.

We should have known that every human mother has the capacity to nurture the seeds of genius within her infant. She has the ability to raise her baby's intelligence to whatever level her own abilities or willingness allow.

We should have known because we have dealt with children and parents for so many years:

Wonderful children who have benefitted hugely from the knowledge, love and respect of their parents.

Potentially wonderful kids, presently average, whose parents and we are determined will not stay average.

Potentially wonderful brain-injured kids

whose parents and we are determined will not stay incapacitated and many of whom are already functioning in an intellectually superior way.

Nose to nose, eye to eye, hand to hand, heart to heart, love to love, worry to worry, joy to joy, success to success, thrill to thrill and sometimes defeat to defeat, but always with determination to determination.

For more than fifty years for the most senior of us.

We are people who *do* things with kids and parents.

We teach *real* parents and *real* children.

We deal in facts not theories.

Our daily reality includes children who are delightful, charming, funny, loving, ordinary, extraordinary, and beguiling. Because they are children, it also at times includes children who are feverish, crying, vomiting, convulsing, dirty-diapered, runny-nosed, hungry and irritable—in short—reality.

When we are reporting how things are in the world of children and using various children as examples, we are dealing with facts. They are real children who have names and addresses and mothers and fathers.

Their many accomplishments are facts not theories.

Looking back, it is not so astonishing how far we have come in our understanding of child development but rather how long it took us to get here.

What we are up to is making each child superior to himself, superior to the way he was yesterday.

In the beginning, the objective was only to make severely brain-injured children who were blind, deaf, paralyzed and speechless able to see, hear, walk and talk. We did this for the next five years, sometimes succeeding, more often failing.

We did it by treating the brain where the problem was rather than in the arms, eyes, legs,and ears, where the symptoms were.

Two things happened.

First—an important number of paralyzed kids got to walk, some blind kids got to see, some deaf kids got to hear, and some speechless kids got to talk.

Second—almost all of those kids had been diagnosed as hopelessly mentally retarded but as they got to walk, and talk, and see and hear, their I.Q.'s went up. Some to average—and some to above average.

It seemed to us that as their I.Q.'s went up, their ability to talk, read, write, do math and function in other ways went up.

It wasn't really until about 1960 that it began to be apparent that that wasn't the way it was at all. That, in fact, it just seemed to be that way.

Even in 1960 it did not hit us like a ton of bricks. It gradually dawned on us with a light that got a little brighter each day. Even today when that light seems crystal clear, it is difficult for us to imagine why it took us so long to understand it and why it isn't apparent to everyone alive that it is true.

It wasn't that as the children became more intelligent they wrote better, read better, did math better, learned better and often performed better than unhurt kids.

It was exactly the opposite.

It was that as children *saw* better, they *read* better; as kids *heard* better, they *understood* better; as kids' ability to *feel* got better, they *moved* better.

In short, it was as children read better, talked better, moved better, and thus took in more and more information—they learned better and their I.Q.s got higher.

Not only was this true of hurt kids but it was true of all kids—average kids and above average kids as well.

The truth is that *intelligence* is a result of *thinking;* it is not that thinking is a result of intelligence.

The truth which we had finally comprehended was soul-stirring to a degree which beggared description.

What we had searched for and at long last stumbled into was nothing less than *the genesis of genius* and that the genesis exists from birth to six.

It was worth the many hundreds of man and woman years we had spent searching for it, and a great deal more.

If intelligence, then, is the result of thinking, and thinking is the genesis of genius, we had better look at intelligence in greater depth.

One thing seems certain and that is that it's good—not bad—to be intelligent.

4

it's good,
not bad,
to be intelligent

*The difference between intelligence
and an education is this—
that intelligence
will make you a good living.*

—CHARLES FRANKLIN KETTERING

I worry a great deal about a world which worships the biceps and which somehow, inexplica-
bly, fears the brain.
As I have the opportunity to go about the world
talking to audiences, I make it a practice to ask
some key questions.
"Do you think it would be good to make our
children stronger?"
Of course it would. The answer is so obvious
as to make the question absurd.

"Do you think it would be good to make our children healthier?"

Of course it would. What a silly question.

"Do you think it would be good to give our children more knowledge?"

Of course. Where are these ridiculous questions leading us?

"Do you think it would be good to make our children more intelligent?"

There is a distinct hesitancy. The audience is divided and slow to respond. Many faces are blank or perturbed. Some heads nod agreement and smile. Most of the smiles are on the faces of the parents of small children.

I have trod on tender toes indeed.

Why in the name of all that is sensible are we humans afraid of high intelligence? It is our human stock-in-trade.

This fear had been epitomized a few years earlier on a B.B.C. television talk show.

We had been talking about what we, through their parents, had been teaching tiny kids.

The host was intelligent, bright-eyed, articulate and warm, but it was obvious that he was becoming increasingly concerned as the conversation progressed. Finally he could stand it no longer.

Host (*accusingly*): But it sounds as if you are proposing some sort of an elite!

We: Precisely.

H: Are you admitting that you propose to create an elite group among children?

W: We are proud of it.

H: Then how many children do you want to have in this elite of yours?

W: About a billion.

H: A billion? How many children are there in the world?

W: About a billion.

H: Aha, now I begin to see—but then, who do you want to make them superior *to*?

W: We want to make them superior to *themselves*.

H: Now, I take your point.

Why must we see high intelligence as a weapon to be used against each other?

What have our geniuses done to us to make us fear them so? Or at all?

What harm did Leonardo da Vinci do us with the *Mona Lisa* or *The Last Supper*?

What harm did Beethoven with his Fifth Symphony?

How were we hurt by Shakespeare with *Henry V*?

How harmed by Franklin with his kite and electricity?

How set back by Michelangelo and his sculpture?

How damaged by Salk and his vaccine which is making polio a forgotten disease ?

How injured by Thomas Jefferson and the Declaration of Independence, which brings tears to my eyes no matter how many times I read it, even though I memorized every word long ago?

How saddened by Gilbert and Sullivan and their *Mikado* which can brighten my dullest day?

How set back by the highly practical Thomas Edison, who knew that genius was one percent inspiration and ninety-nine percent perspiration and who was there with me the last time I lived with a Bushman tribe in the Kalihari Desert, brightening my darkest night with a bare electric light bulb powered by a little generator?

The list is endless and stretches across the nations and the oceans and back into the ages through time unremembered. It includes the geniuses remembered, and unknown, in every nation and place.

Write your own list. Who are your favorite geniuses and what harm did they do you?

Ah! Favorite geniuses. What about the hated

geniuses? Do I hear a voice or a chorus ask—
what about the evil geniuses of history? Do I
hear a note of triumph as some asks, "What
about Hitler?"

Evil genius, my foot.

It is a contradiction in terms.

Try mass-murderer if you need a description
of Hitler and all his ilk throughout history.
Does it take high intelligence to incite mass insanity in man, a creature who was a club-wield-
ing, skulking predator called *Australopithecus
Afrikanus Dartii* only days ago as the geologists
measure time?

Hitler was a failure by his own standard, never
mind by mine. Is it the goal of genius to end up
lying on a wet concrete floor doused with gaso-
line and lit by his own order? Was it Hitler's
goal to die with Germany in ruin around his
own charred corpse?

Genius is as genius does.

We are stuck with the paradox of the evil genius only if we are determined to rely upon ar-
chaic definitions of genius measured by absurd
tests of intelligence.

The mad genius and the bumbling ineffective
genius are a product of the same perspective.
They are nothing more and nothing less than a
monumental mistake in the measurement of
intelligence.

Why do we abide definitions which are on the face of them—absurd?

To stop fearing genius we need only measure it by its accomplishments.

Do we fear the term "elite" which means "the best of a group"? Only, apparently, when it applies to intelligence. Is it a sin to be physically elite? Not on your life.

We fear intelligence and worship muscle.

Periodically we go joyfully through a process which proclaims it throughout the world and to all the inhabitants thereof.

This process culminates when we place three young adults on boxes of three different heights and place a medal around the neck of each of them. We then proclaim them to be the *crème de la crème*, the three most elite of the elite. This young lady can jump higher than anyone in the world. This young man can run faster than anyone in the world. Hearts beat high, eyes gleam with tears and bosoms swell with pride as each flag is raised and each national anthem is played. And if that particular flag and that particular anthem happen to be mine, it is joy almost beyond enduring.

Do I then disclaim this elitism beyond all elitism which we call the Olympics?

No, of course not. I think it's fine. It is first

rate that our young athletes should be physically superior.

We believe that all children should be physically excellent.

Indeed we teach parents precisely how to make them so.

I worry a good deal about a world which worships muscles and fears intelligence.

In my life I have walked down many dark streets, late at night and alone, in many countries. Never once in my life—as I passed a pool of blackness which hid a dark alley—have I been afraid that someone would leap out of the blackness . . . and say something bright to me.

Or ask me a brilliant question.

Have you?

On the other hand I have worried, times beyond counting, that three hundred pounds of biceps might leap out and demolish me.

I worry about a world that worships muscle and fears intelligence.

I can't help wondering at each presidential election whether the world is worried that the republican or democratic candidate is *too* intelligent.

Is not our fear exactly the opposite?

Has anyone ever worried that our senators or representatives might be too bright?

Or is it that we feared that our leaders might

not be wise enough? The world rocked with laughter a decade or so ago when a member of the U.S. Congress proposed that what we needed in government was more mediocrity, thus establishing that what we had was less than mediocre. Should we have laughed—or cried?

It's good, not bad, to be intelligent.

Indeed, it's very good.

5

heredity, environment and intelligence

If in fact it's good to be intelligent, then it behooves us to know something about intelligence.

What intelligence is, and where it comes from, has always been a subject of lively, if not always sensible, debate which has taken place from ancient Grecian courtyards to today's college classrooms.

Twenty-five hundred years ago, ancient

Empedocles believed that the heart was the seat of thought and intelligence, while that genius Hippocrates, teaching his medical students under his plane tree on the island of Cos, taught them that the human brain was the organ which contained and controlled intelligence.

It seems fascinating to me that the ancient Greeks' vast respect for their great men and women caused them to be called "gods" after their deaths. Thus the Greeks, among whom there were so many geniuses, created their own gods.

So it was that Asclepius, the physician who lived twelve centuries before Christ, became the God Asclepius after his death.

Today we carry out much the same practice, but we have changed the name. Today we observe people whose brilliance and sometimes godlike characteristics set them apart—and call them geniuses. Like the Greeks, we often wait till after their death to give them the title they earned in life.

As the twentieth century draws to a close we have, at long last, resolved the question of where intelligence lies. It lies in the brain. What is still hotly debated is the question of whence cometh this intelligence.

Today the debate which rages is whether this

intelligence is hereditary in nature or whether it is environmental.

Is it nature or nurture?

This divides the world into two schools of thought.

There are the hereditary people and the environment people.

Both schools are dead certain they are right.

Both sides are absolutely sure that these views are mutually exclusive.

Both sides use the same argument to prove they are right.

I am, myself, a good example of both points of view.

Kind people refer to me as "portly." The truth is I am a bit fat.

The heredity people look at me and say, "He is too heavy. No doubt his parents are too heavy." Sure enough, my father and my mother were a bit portly. Thus they conclude it is entirely hereditary.

The environment people say that my parents ate too much and therefore taught me to eat too much, with the result that I am a bit portly. Thus they conclude it is entirely environmental.

In this case, the environment people are right.

Surely the hereditary people are right in believing that my eyes and my hair and my height and my build are an inheritance from my parents, grandparents and great-grandparents—but my weight?

While I'd very much like to blame that on my grandparents, in truth I can't.

Twice in my life I was thin—very thin. Several times as a combat infantry officer during World War II, I managed (or mismanaged) to get myself behind German lines for periods of time. The *Wehrmacht*, understandably, tended to be inhospitable towards that sort of thing. I grew thin.

At the University of Pennsylvania I earned no scholarships and ate less well than I might have chosen. Then also I grew thin.

On the other hand, during most of my life I have enjoyed fine food, with the result that kind people have called me "stocky."

It hardly seems necessary to point out that my grandmother's weight did not go up and down during the periods when I ate too little or too much.

Function determines structure.

I'd love to blame my fatness on grandfather Ricker or grandmother McCarthy—but it won't wash.

There is in the world a very small group of people who do not see heredity and environment as being the mutually exclusive cause of what we are, or can become. We are among that group.

How much then can be said for these points of view?

Come with me for a quick trip around the world to visit groups of children doing extraordinary things, a trip we have actually made a number of times. Let's see whether these particular children are a product of environment or of heredity.

Let's try first to make a case for heredity.

Come with me to Melbourne and back in time to the late 1960s. We find ourselves in a large indoor swimming pool and behold a charming sight. In the pool are twenty or thirty beautiful pink tiny babies, ranging in age from a few weeks old to a year old. They are accompanied by beautiful pink mothers in bikinis. The babies are learning to swim; indeed, they are swimming.

There is a two-year-old boy who insists I throw him into the deep water. He swims out and insists that I do it again and again. I tire of throwing him in before he tires of swimming out.

There is a three-year-old girl who is working on her Red Cross Life-Saving Badge. She tows her mother across the pool.

Today everyone knows that infants can easily be taught to swim, but this was in the late sixties.

I am delighted but somehow not surprised. Why should newborns not swim? They have, after all, been swimming for nine months.

At the end of the session, the mothers go to dress their babies and themselves. They return carrying their babies in large baby baskets or in their arms. I am agog. The tiny babies can swim but they can't walk!

I learned to swim at nine years of age in the North Philadelphia Y.M.C.A. Everybody I knew learned to swim in the Y.M.C.A. at nine years of age. Ergo—everybody learns to swim at nine years of age.

Since I knew that everyone learns to swim at nine, it followed that anyone I saw swimming was at least nine years old. Subtly, in order to justify my firmly held belief, I had subconsciously resolved the dilemma between what I saw and what I believed. I had concluded that these infants were nine-year-old midgets. Only the fact that they had to be carried forced me to deal consciously with this patent absurdity.

We shall return to Australia and try to make a case for heredity.

Now, off to Tokyo, and back in time to the early 1970s. We find ourselves in the Early Development Association of Japan.

Again we are treated to a charming sight. Kneeling in the middle of a large room are two young women. One is American, the other Japanese. Kneeling in a semi-circle around them are a score of Japanese mothers, each with a tiny child in her lap. Most of the children are two years old; some of them are three.

The American speaks to the first tiny child in English, "Fumio, what is your address?"

Fumio answers in full and clear and understandable English. He has a faint Philadelphia accent.

Fumio then turns to the little girl occupying the lap next to him and asks, "Mitsue, how many brothers and sisters do you have?"

Mitsue answers, "Two brothers and two sisters."

Mitsue also has just a touch of a Philadelphia accent, but only a Philadelphian would know it. She now turns to the little girl on the next lap and asks her, "Michiko, what is your telephone number?"

"Five, three, nine, one, six, three, five, five," responds Michiko.

Michiko turns to the little boy to her left and asks, "Jun, is there a tree in front of your house?"

"There is a ginko tree in a hole in the pavement."

Jun, like all the children, has a faint Japanese accent and the word "hole" sounds faintly like "hore." When he says the word "pavement" it sounds just a little as if he had said "payment." To a Bostonian, that would scream "Philadelphia."

Neither my wife Katie nor I was in the least surprised at this beguiling scene because, of course, the American teacher was our daughter, Janet Doman, who is now the director of the Institutes.

Her Japanese assistant was Miki Nakayachi, who was to become the instructor of Japanese at the Institutes and later the first director of our International School.

But now it is time to tear ourselves away from this enticing scene and visit another equally enchanting scene to meet one of the greatest teachers of this or any century.

Come with us several hundred miles to the northwest of Tokyo to a venerable mountain town in the Japanese alps called Matsumoto and meet its most famous citizen, Shinichi Suzuki.

For a decade before our first meeting, Professor Suzuki had known of our work and we had known of his. Strangely, the first man who told us of Suzuki's work didn't believe it and we did. I remember with amusement the heated discussion that followed.

Looking back on the debate it seems absurd that I should have been defending with passion a man I had never heard of half an hour earlier, and that he should be attacked with vitriol by a man who knew nothing about him except that (it was said) he taught two- and three-year-olds to play the violin.

The reason for the verbal fisticuffs was simple enough. Although neither of us had ever seen a three-year-old play the violin I was dead certain it *could* be done and he was equally certain that it *could not* be done.

At the Institutes we had learned that children were linguistic geniuses who dealt with learning English without the slightest effort.

English has a 450,000 word vocabulary. The number of ways in which those words can be combined is not, in fact, infinite, but it will do until infinity comes along.

Music is also a language but it has seven notes not 450,000. If the ways in which these notes can be combined seems endless, it docs not approach the number of ways in which 450,000 words can be combined.

Since tiny children are able to learn English with its vast vocabulary so easily, then it should be easier for them to learn the language of music.

In fact, you can teach little children anything that you can present to them in an honest and factual way.

Why shouldn't a man named Suzuki have discovered how to teach children to play the violin in an honest and factual way?

The answer to that question was simple.

He had.

Suzuki has taught, directly or indirectly, more than 100,000 tiny children to play the violin.

Now, finally, we were going to meet Dr. Suzuki and his little violinists.

We met as old friends. What a gentle genius he is. His love and respect for his tiny children shines through everything he says and does.

Come with us into the lovely auditorium draped with banners, welcoming us to Matsumoto.

What a thrilling thing to hear for the first time the absolute glory of these little children in concert. We were prepared to hear them play and to play well. We were not prepared for the actuality. That first concert filled, then flooded, and finally overwhelmed our senses.

We would hear them many times again.

We would have the great pleasure of hearing more than five thousand Suzuki students at their Annual National Concert in Tokyo.

The opportunity to enjoy thousands of very young children playing Mozart, Bach and Beethoven in concert is an experience which defies description.

It is surely one of the most compelling and persuasive proofs that tiny children can indeed learn anything that can be taught to them in a loving and honest way.

We have also heard ten of them, ranging in age from three to ten, play at Philadelphia's Academy of Music, the home of the Philadelphia Orchestra. The Institutes have sponsored these concerts over the years.

Philadelphia music audiences are not the most demonstrative in the world. They are appreciative but not demonstrative. We have filled the Academy with music lovers paying the same prices as those charged when the Philadelphia Orchestra plays. These little children have never failed to receive a heartfelt and completely deserved standing ovation.

Let's get back to our trip around the world.

Come with me back half a lifetime to 1943 and the Infantry Officer Candidate School at Fort Benning, Georgia.

In one of the alphabetically arranged bunks we find officer candidate John Eaglebull, full-blooded Sioux, college-educated and hereditary chief among his tribe. Next to him we find officer candidate Glenn Doman. "D"—Doman, "E"—Eaglebull.

In the grueling but neatly ordered and exciting months that followed, we became close friends, although Eaglebull tended to be as stoic as his handsome Indian face suggested him to be.

I was therefore surprised when he casually mentioned his son. I had known he was married, but this was the first time I knew he had a son.

Out came his wallet and the inevitable photograph.

"My son," said Eaglebull, rather majestically.

The snapshot made me shudder. Here, seated on a full-grown horse, was a very handsome little two-and-a-half-year-old boy. He looked to be a mile in the air. No adult held him; he was bare-back and held the reins. His little legs did not hang down the sides of the horse, they stuck out so that you could see the bottom of his feet.

"Good Lord, Eaglebull, what a dangerous thing for you to do."

"Why is it dangerous to take a photograph, Doman?"

"Suppose the horse had moved while you were taking the picture?"

"Would have ruined the snapshot."

"Eaglebull, he would have fractured his skull."

Before I enlisted in the Army my job had been fixing up hurt brains and the thought of that little boy falling off a horse on his head horrified me.

The puzzlement on Eaglebull's strong face made his answer slow in coming. When what I was protesting became clear, his answer was indignant.

"That's *his* horse," said Eaglebull. "I don't know anybody who can remember when he couldn't ride a horse, any more than you know anybody who can remember when he couldn't walk."

In my mind's ear I could hear tom-toms beating.

Eaglebull's father still bore the scars he had earned while dancing the Sun Dance. My own grandmother had been a small girl when Custer had died at the Little Big Horn.

James Warner Bellah, the great authority on the cavalry-Indian wars, had once described the Sioux as "five thousand of the world's finest light cavalry."

Of course they were the world's finest light cavalry. Why shouldn't they have been? They were born on horses.

Come to Philadelphia and the Institutes in 1965 for our final group of little children. On one side of Stenton Avenue sits Philadelphia, proud of its three hundred years of history, of its art museum, its orchestra, its many universities, its seven medical schools, its beautiful suburbs.

Philadelphia remembers its position as the first capital of the United States, at which time it was second only to London as the largest English-speaking city in the world.

Yet in its modern school system, one third of all the children from seven to seventeen couldn't read, or couldn't read at grade level (which actually means the same thing). Not only was it possible, and still is, to graduate from high school without being able to read your own diploma, but students still do, every term.

Before your bosom swells with pride as you compare your own city to Philadelphia, have a close look at the facts in your city.

Yet just across Stenton Avenue, eleven feet away, in Montgomery County, lies the campus of the Institutes for the Achievement of Human Potential. Even in 1965 the Institutes had hundreds of brain-injured two- and three-year-old children who could read with total understanding. What in the world could it mean?

What does it all mean?

Two-month-old babies who could swim; in fact, lots of them.

Japanese children, not yet four years old, carrying on conversations in English, with a Philadelphia accent.

Japanese kids, not yet four years old, who could play the violin, some of them giving concerts and playing solos at Philadelphia's Academy of Music for highly sophisticated audiences.

Sioux children, hardly more than babies, riding horses—all of them.

Two- and three-year-old brain-injured kids, ranging from mild to profound, who can read with understanding, while a third of well ones ranging in age from seven to seventeen, can't.

Is it heredity or is it environment?

Let's first try to make a case for heredity.

Back we go to Australia and the infants who swim. Heredity? Maybe.

Take a look at a map of Australia. Four thousand miles of gorgeous beaches and beautiful warm seas. What a marvelous place to swim (if you don't mind the odd shark).

Perhaps, with all those glorious beaches, the Australians, over thousands of years, tens of thousands of years, have developed some ancient genetic predisposition for swimming which gives them a hereditary genetic advantage over the rest of us.

Do I hear a clear-thinking Australian saying, "Hold on a minute, what do you mean, ten thousand years? We haven't been here a thousand years. Only the aborigines have been here one thousand years, and most of them have never seen enough water to swim in. Can't swim if you haven't had enough water to swim in, can you now? Not even 'strylians can do that. We're a bunch of transplanted Englishmen, Scots, Welshmen and Irishmen."

Do I hear another voice, a bit less strident (perhaps a biologist) saying, "Come off it. Don't talk to me about genetic change in a thousand years, or fifty thousand. A hundred thousand maybe."

What is it then, if not genetic?

Those Australian babies were swimming twenty years ago because a couple of Australians thought that little babies ought to be able to swim, and proved it.

Come to think of it, that couple was actually Dutch! If they'd stayed in Holland, it would have been a bunch of Dutch babies who would have been swimming and we'd have gone to Holland to see them. That couple was the environment.

What about those Japanese kids speaking English? . . . Is that heredity?

Everybody knows how clever the Japanese are and how concerned they are about their children. Perhaps the Japanese, speaking English for thousands of years have developed a genetic. . . .

"Wait a minute," I can hear everybody shouting, "How could the Japanese have been speaking English a thousand years ago when not a single Englishman had ever. . . ."

Okay, okay. So it isn't heredity. Then what is it?

We had known for a long time that all kids are linguistic geniuses and that to a Japanese baby born in Tokyo today, Japanese is a foreign language. No more and no less than is English. Does anyone doubt that he'll speak Japanese before he's four?

The Institutes' English-speaking staff were the environment of those Japanese kids. How else can we explain those faint Philadelphia accents we heard in the Japanese kids?

What about the Suzuki children playing the violin superbly? Isn't that heredity? Everybody knows how clever the Japanese are with their hands. Isn't it possible that the Japanese playing the violins for thous—.

Wait, I'd better not start that stuff again. Let's see, Admiral Perry got to Japan about 150 years ago and. . . .

Well, if it isn't genetic, then what is it?

It is a man, a genius, called Shinichi Suzuki, who thought that tiny children ought to be able to play the violin, and except for Suzuki himself, there is nothing either Japanese or hereditary about it.

Now little children in every corner of the globe play the violin and—come to think of it, Eugene Ormandy was playing it at two, and how long ago did Yehudi Menuhin start to play the violin—or Mozart?

And those 5,000 children at the national concert, playing those fine old Japanese composers—Mozart, Vivaldi and Bach?

The Australians have no corner on swimming.

Nor do the Japanese on speaking English.

Nor do the Japanese on violin playing.

Hold on, Doman, what about the Sioux kids riding horses? Didn't you yourself say that they were born on horses?

Yes, I did say that and perhaps in this case it is hereditary.

Suppose that the Indians putting their babies on horses since time immemorial has. . . .

Stop!

I can hear the history student laughing out loud.

"There were no horses in the New World until the Conquistadores came." Eighteen Spaniards and eighteen horses swept the highly civilized Aztecs before them in their thousands, and later the brilliant Incas, who were doing successful brain surgery before ever a white man set foot in the New World.

Civilized though they were, they were laden

with superstitions. They had never seen a horse. When they saw a horse and rider separate into two parts, they came to the conclusion that these were gods. They kneeled down to worship them and they died by the thousands.

Not until the Conquistadores started to cross the great deserts of what is now the American southwest did they know defeat, for there they ran into the Apache.

The Apache did not think they were gods, but men, riding a new kind of animal. The Apache killed them and took their horses.

Horses were ideally suited to the North American Indians and horses spread among the Indians and eventually got to the Sioux.

We shall not go through the business of genes or heredity again. Horses quickly became part of the Sioux environment, far less than three hundred years ago.

The Sioux children have no corner on riding horses. Any child alive can be an expert horse-man—all he needs is to be given the opportunity, and the earlier he is given it, the better horseman he will be.

The Sioux children begin riding horses at one day of age—albeit in their mothers' arms.

How about the tiny brain-injured children at the Institutes in Philadelphia reading with understanding at two and three years of age—while across the street one-third of the well children from age seven to age seventeen cannot.

Is that genetics? Well some people have proposed that these brain-injured children are special genetically, but special bad, not special good.

In fact they are not special genetically either bad or good—they are brain-injured. But one wonders if anyone thinks it's an advantage to be brain-injured?

The truth is that all children are linguistic geniuses—and as a result the staff has taught their mothers to teach them to read.

That's environmental.

There now, we people of the Institutes seem to have come down squarely on the side of the environmentalist, and indeed we have.

Do heredity and genetics then, have nothing to do with intelligence?

Lord, they have everything to do with it.

6

Homo sapiens, the gift of genes

*If I appear to see further
than others it is because
I sit on the shoulders of
giants.*

—Baron Gottfried Wilhelm
von Leibwitz (1646-1716)

The problem about understanding heredity is that we've got our species, *Homo sapiens,* mixed up with our families such as Smiths, Joneses, McShains, Buckners, Matsuzawas, Verases, Samotos and so on through the clans.

We've got it in our heads that from a hereditary standpoint we can't rise above what the last four or five generations of our family made us capable of being genetically.

Aside from some not very important physical

characteristics such as color of hair and general body structure, which we've already discussed, the rest, I submit, doesn't matter.

The idea that I can't rise above what my grandfather or grandmother was, and that you can't rise above yours, is foolish enough to be silly.

My Irish grandmother died before I was born so I know little about her, but I do remember my grandmother Ricker. She was a nice, God-fearing, straight-laced farm lady, and the idea that I can't rise in an intellectual way above what she and grandfather Ricker or grandfather Doman was is not worth discussing at any length.

Do you know who would be totally repulsed by such an idea? My grandparents, that's who.

My grandparents spent their entire lives arranging for their children to stand on their shoulders. They arranged for their children to begin where they left off. It was their goal in life.

My parents' first goal in life was for me to stand on their shoulders. To start where they left off.

And our goal in life has been, and is, for our children to stand on our shoulders and to start where we leave off.

We're blessed with a very large family, at least

in a spiritual sense: the entire staff of the
Institutes. I am forced to say they're doing a
magnificent job.

If Temple Fay should return to the Institutes
from that teaching heaven where he presently
resides and sit in the auditorium of the building which is named for him (how I wish he
could) and listen to the youngest staff member,
it would take him a while to understand what
was being taught. He would listen attentively,
and then, being the genius that he was, a great
smile would light his face and he would say,
"Yes. Of course. I should have known that."

For the youngest staff member in the
Institutes knows more about children and how
their brains grow than Temple Fay knew in his
entire life.

Conversely, if Dr. Fay could now sit in the
same auditorium and listen to me teach, and if
he heard me say only those hundreds of brilliant things he had taught me, a slowly increas-
ing frown would cross his face and he would
say, "I picked the wrong young man to teach.
He didn't stand on my shoulders, he sat on my
lap."

Temple Fay was probably the greatest brain
surgeon that ever lived with the possible exception of Hippocrates (considering how long ago
Hippocrates lived).

There are tens of thousands of people alive, perhaps more, who would be dead were it not for Fay's invention of human refrigeration.

His reward was to be attacked by virtually the entire world.

Long after Fay's death, I find great pleasure in watching the faces of parents of children who were in automobile accidents and whose lives were saved by hypothermia as those parents listen to lectures in the auditorium of the Temple Fay Building.

Today there is no hospital which would dare call itself modern which doesn't have one or more departments using human refrigeration.

We, all of us, stood on the shoulders of that giant Temple Fay and he did not find our feet pressing into his shoulders to be uncomfortable. He liked how they felt.

Don't you like the feeling of your children's feet on your shoulders?

Why else would you ever have picked up a book called *How to Multiply Your Baby's Intelligence*?

One wonders if the universal custom which fathers have of putting their children on their shoulders, a habit beloved of fathers and beloved of children, isn't a lot more than just pleasant play.

The ability of having our children begin

where we left off is a uniquely human characteristic. It is a product of the wondrous and unique human cortex.

It is what, of all things, most characterizes we human beings, what separates us from the great apes and all the rest of God's creatures.

Every chimpanzee born is doomed to live, step for step, the same life as his father's before him. He is predestined to be a chimpanzee, which means he can learn only what his parents can teach him, or at most, what the other members of the tribe can teach him. They pay a great deal of attention and they teach their young most earnestly. They do a first-rate job and as a result he grows into a first-rate chimpanzee.

Not so with us.

Well, I can hear you say, isn't that what happens to us? Doesn't this very book propose that we must make our children into first-rate human beings?

Of course it does. But a first-rate chimpanzee is a stable thing, a creature which if it changes in any significant way will change over eons of time.

Not so with human beings.

Oh, how we change. We are not stable creatures.

Nor are we confined to what our grandparents were.

When humans, with our ingenious brains, invented written abstract languages, our ability to change multiplied a thousand times.

No longer were we confined to what our parents could teach us. Not by a long shot. For that moment when first we learned to read set us free.

Free!

No longer were we confined to what our parents could teach us. For example, now we could read whatever glorious thing was written in the English language, all the golden things that every brilliant or funny or warm or delightful man or woman ever wrote in English.

Free also to learn any other language, which is why it's great to teach babies to understand, speak, read and write several languages.

Don't you remember the very day that you really learned to read?

You must have had the same experience that I had.

Mother had been reading to me since before I could remember and she had always held the book in my lap as I sat on her lap. As a consequence I knew all the words.

Don't you remember when your mother skipped a word or a sentence or a page as her eyes grew heavy. How you said, "No, Mommy, it doesn't say that, it says—."

I was five or thereabouts. It was a rainy day and I couldn't go out so Mother said, "Lie down on the floor and read a book. Here's a new one. When you find a word you don't know, come out in the kitchen and I'll tell you what is says."

So I did.

I read on and on. I found myself growing excited. Suddenly it hit me like a ton of bricks. I knew why I was excited. The person who had written this book was talking to *me.* He was telling me something I never knew before. I had it. I had what every little kid in the world wants more than anything else. I had captured my own adult and he couldn't get away. He didn't have to do the laundry, or turn off the peas or put out the ashes. He was mine.

That's when it all began. I read everything I could get my hands on whether I could read it or not. Mother or Dad was always there to tell me what it said.

Isn't mother the environment too?

Of course she is the environment of the child and except for father she is practically the only thing in it.

So where's the great hereditary gift that the title of this chapter proposes that this chapter is going to tell you about?

Who's your favorite genius? Edison?

Beethoven? Mark Twain? Socrates? Gainsborough? Einstein? Shakespeare? Bach? Pauling? Salk? Picasso? Vivaldi?

Do you know that you are directly related to your favorite genius?

Nobody ever saw a German gene or a French gene or an Italian gene or a Japanese gene or, most certainly, an American gene.

When Einstein died we took his brain and it's been examined ever since.

We're trying to find out how it's different from yours and mine.

No luck so far.

Good luck to those who are trying. It doesn't have any German characteristics or Princeton genes or atomic genes, although in life it was all full of German knowledge and Princeton knowledge and $E=MC^2$ or whatever it was.

It is shockingly like your brain in every important way, for Einstein was given the brain of *Homo sapiens* and that's exactly the potential that your brain had at birth.

It had a glorious gift. It had the genes of *Homo sapiens* and that's precisely what yours had and what your baby's has.

I must admit to being proud of being a Doman, and a staff member of the Institutes, and a Philadelphian, and a Pennsylvanian, and an American, and a citizen of the world, for I am all those things. Just as I am sure that you are proud of all the things you are, we are justifiably proud of who we are.

But they are not the greatest thing we are—not by a million miles. Nor are we confined to being what the other members of those groups are or were.

We human beings are confined to being *Homo sapiens*—and nothing else.

We are confined to being human beings.

We may be anything that any human being is.

We may be anything that any human being ever was.

We may be anything that any human being may be. For every human being has the gift of the genes of *Homo sapiens.*

If this has begun to sound like an inspirational message such as those delivered by Norman Vincent Peale and all the other fine people who exhort us, very properly, to make the most of what we've got, well fine, and I certainly believe we should.

But that is not at all what I'm really saying. What I'm saying is not an inspirational message, it is a biological and neurological message.

The kind of human being we are going to be, whether exceptional, average or slow; whether kindly, humane, stern, mean or cruel; whether inspired or ordinary, is largely determined by six years of age.

At birth the child is an unwritten book with the potential to be anything that any human being ever was or is, or may ever be. He remains so until six.

So we do have a genetic gift. We are born with the greatest gift we could possibly be given. We all of us have the genes of *Homo sapiens*.

Now let's talk about kids and the first six years of life.

7

everything
Leonardo learned

What is a three-year-old really like as opposed to the way we adults believe him to be?

Babies are born with a rage to learn. They want to learn about everything and they want to learn about it right now.

Tiny kids think that learning is the greatest thing that ever happened. The world spends the first six years of life trying to tell them that learning isn't the greatest thing in life and that playing is.

Some kids never learn that playing is the

greatest thing in life and as a result those kids go all the way through life believing that learning is the greatest thing in life. Those are the ones we call geniuses.

Babies think that learning is a survival skill—and so it is.

Learning is a survival skill and it's very dangerous to be very young and helpless.

It takes 10,000 trout eggs to produce a single surviving trout, 40 turtle eggs to produce an adult turtle. Turtle eggs are very vulnerable to predators; the tiny turtles heading down the beach to the sea are in great danger. After they make it safely into the sea they face new predators.

The dead baby squirrels and rabbits one sees along the road in early summer that didn't live long enough to learn how to survive are mute evidence to a stern law of nature — learning is a survival skill.

This is especially true in human beings, and every baby knows it. It is built into him.

Nature has brilliant tricks for insuring the survival of both the race and the individual.

To insure the survival of the race she plays a charming and delightful trick on us. It's called sex. Have you ever paused to think about what the population of the world would be if sex were unpleasant and painful? And how long ago the population would have been zero?

Upon each individual baby born she plays her trick to insure his survival. She has him born believing that learning is the absolutely best thing that ever happened and every child born does believe it and will forever unless we talk him out of it or badger him out of it—or both.

You mustn't take our word for this; it's far too important. If you want to know what three-year-olds *really* think, instead of the nonsense we tell each other they think, (patty-cake and all of that) why don't you consult a real authority on three-year-olds? Why don't you ask a three-year-old?

When you ask him be willing to listen to him through clear ears and to look at him through clear eyes. If you know what he's going to say before he says it you'll hear him say what you *thought* he was going to say and see him do what you *thought* he was going to do.

Remember the power of myths.

Ask a three-year-old what he really wants. If he trusts you, you won't get a chance to ask him; he'll ask you. He won't ask you how three-year-olds are—he knows all about that. He'll ask you endless questions, as everyone knows, thus proving that three-year-olds don't want to play patty-cake—they want to learn.

(The great advantage to being unreasonable,

as all myth makers are, is that you can hold two opposing views simultaneously. Ergo—*everybody knows* that little kids want to play and everybody knows that little kids ask questions endlessly).

The truth is that little kids don't want to play and that they do ask an unending series of questions—and what superb questions they are.

"Daddy, what holds the stars up in the sky?"

"Mommy, why is the grass green?"

"Daddy, how does the little man get into the television set?"

Those are brilliant questions—precisely the same questions that top flight scientists ask.

Our answer, in one way or another, is, "Look kid, Daddy is very busy deciding what we ought to do in the Middle East situation so he can write a letter to the editor and tell him what to do. Why don't you run off and play while Daddy thinks."

There are two reasons that we never answer his questions.

The first reason we don't is that we know he wouldn't understand the answer if we did tell him.

The second reason is that we don't know the answers to his questions. They are brilliant questions.

Since 1962 every American has paid one cent out of every tax dollar to support that genius organization called NASA. They can take a dime out of my tax dollar anytime they want.

It isn't that I am so enthusiastic about being on the moon. But the ability to *get* to the moon, and even more the ability to *get back*—well that's incredible.

If somebody asked you to sum up the entire space program in a single, simple, clear question and gave you a year to decide on what that question should be, do you think you could come up with a shorter, simpler, clearer question than, "What holds the stars up in the sky?"

Or, "What makes the grass green Daddy?"

The truth is I don't know.

"Come on Glenn, you know what makes the grass green."

"Chlorophyll—honey, chlorophyll makes the grass green."

"Daddy, why doesn't chlorophyll make the grass red?"

And there the kid has got me because I don't really know why chlorophyll makes the grass green.

Unless you are a biologist I suspect you don't either.

So mother says, "Because, honey."

One of our devoted professional mothers, who really does respect her child, told me the following story.

She had been asked a question by her tiny daughter and, as always, it was a brilliant question. Because she is a splendid mother she was trying to frame a clear answer to her child's question and her daughter grew impatient.

"Why, Mommy?—*Because?*

Mother was horrified.

We should all think about that.

"Daddy, how did the little man get in the television set?"

That question has been bugging me ever since I first saw the little man in the television set and most particularly since each of our own tiny children, in turn, asked me that question.

I could bluff my way through that question with one minute on light waves and one minute on sound waves but it wouldn't work.

The fact is I don't really know.

As a result I never tried to answer the question beyond saying, "I don't know." I never lie to children or try to fool them.

I lie to myself and fool myself once in awhile. But I never lie to children or try to fool them.

It never works because children, especially tiny children, see through adults more clearly than they see through glass windows.

All tiny kids see through all adults.

No adult should ever try to fool a child because it never works, and I at least am too old to do things that don't work—I haven't got time.

Back to the little man in the television set.

People my age are fascinated by television. We weren't born in a world full of television sets or a sky full of airplanes as today's kids are. Would you believe that when I hear an airplane I look up?

It isn't the garbage on the television set which fascinates us, it's the electronic miracle.

It's the question of how the little man got in the television set. Us and tiny kids.

What do we, in fact, do when our children ask us one of those brilliant and impossible-to-answer questions

What we actually do is say, "Look kid, here's a rattle (or a toy truck depending on whether the child is a year old or three years old). Go play with it."

Marshall McLuhan used to say that miniaturization is an art form much appreciated by adults.

It is lost on kids who must think we are as crazy as Hoot Owls.

"This is a truck?" says the three-year-old to himself as he holds it in his small hand.

"They told me that trucks were those giant things that rattle the windows as they pass and feel hot and smell greasy and which will squash you if you get in front of them. *This* is a truck?"

Little kids have solved that kind of grown-up dichotomy. They had to.

They say, "They're bigger than me so if they call this a truck, I'll call it a truck."(Thank goodness kids are linguistic geniuses).

What happens when we give the small child a toy truck?

Well, everybody knows what happens. He "plays" with it for a minute and a half and then he gets bored and throws it away.

We notice this and have a ready explanation: he has a short attention span. I'm big and I have a long attention span and he's little so he has a short attention span. Big brain, little brain.

How arrogant we are, and how blind. We saw exactly what we thought we were going to see.

May we go back and watch again, but this time may we see what really happened?

We have just *seen* a brilliant demonstration of how kids learn, but we think it's a demonstration of how kids are inferior.

Tiny children have just five ways to learn about the world. They can see it, hear it, feel it, taste it and smell it.

No more.

Five laboratory tests available to learn about the world. And that is exactly the same number as Leonardo had. So too do you and I. Five ways to learn.

Let's play it back. We gave the child the rattle or toy truck which he had never seen before. If he had seen it before he would simply have thrown it away immediately and demanded something he hadn't seen before. This is why basements fill up with junk called toys which children "played" with once and refused to look at again.

So we give him a new toy in the hope that this will get his attention.

First he looked at it (which is why toys are painted bright colors).

Next he listened to it (which is why toys make noises).

Next he felt it (which is why toys don't have sharp edges).

Then he tasted it (which is why toys are made with non-poisonous materials).

Finally he smells it (we haven't figured out how toys should smell yet so they don't smell).

That clever and discerning process of using every laboratory test available to him to learn everything there is worth learning about this piece of junk called a toy takes about sixty seconds.

But the child is not only clever, he is ingenious. There is one more thing he might learn. He might learn how it is put together by breaking it apart.

So he tries to break it. It takes about thirty seconds for him to find that he can't break it. So he throws it away. This, of course, is why toys are unbreakable.

It's one of two methods we adults employ for the prevention of learning;

First there is the make-it-so-he-can't-break-it school of thought for the prevention of learning.

The second is the put-him-in-the-playpen-where-he-can't-get-at-it school of thought.

He's trying desperately to learn and we're trying desperately to get him to play.

He actually succeeds, despite us, in learning all there is to learn about the toy and since he never did want to play he promptly throws it away.

The whole process takes ninety seconds.

We watch that absolutely brilliant performance and use it to prove he's inferior.

The question is, "How long should anybody look at a rattle?"

The answer should be, "As long as there's something to learn from it."

If that is the right answer then I can tell you that I've never seen any adult do it as brilliantly as a three-year-old.

There are five pathways into the brain—and only five.

Everything a child learns in his life he learns through those five paths. He can see it, hear it, feel it, taste it and smell it.

Everything that Leonardo learned he learned through those five pathways.

8
all kids are
linguistic geniuses

When it comes to kids there is no end to adult arrogance.

It's that old dehydrated adult myth again.

Little kids aren't as big as me, they aren't as heavy as me and they aren't as bright as me.

Not as big as me? True.

Not as heavy as me? Certainly true.

Not as bright as me? Ho, ho, ho.

There is no more difficult intellectual task for an adult than trying to learn a foreign language. A very small percentage of grown-ups ever succeed in speaking a foreign tongue fluently. The number of adults who succeed in speaking a foreign language flawlessly and without a trace of accent is so small as to be insignificant. The infinitely small number of adults who learn a foreign language as adults are the subject of almost universal admiration and envy.

I would rather speak a foreign tongue fluently than perform any other intellectual act in the world. I would like to speak Portuguese, Japanese or Italian—but I'll take anything. I have lived for brief or extended periods in more than a hundred countries but I cannot utter a coherent or grammatically correct sentence in any foreign tongue, never mind with a proper accent. It isn't that I haven't tried. I've tried very hard.

I've got phrase books in fifty languages and I use them. At least I try. Nobody expects the English or Americans to even try. When you do try they find it charming. The worse you are, the more charming they find it to be.

I'm extremely charming.

I get into a French cab and I say something like, "Me—taxi—hotel."

The cab driver glances over his shoulder and says, "Where do you want to go, Jack, to the hotel?"

He says it with an American accent. He's a bit younger than I. So I know that he was a kid during the American invasion and that he was in the American Zone.

If any adult wants to get a quick inferiority complex all he has to do is to get himself into a language learning contest with any eighteen-month-old.

Suppose we took a brilliant thirty-year-old who was at once a Rhodes scholar and an Olympic Gold Medal winner at the height of his prowess. Suppose we said to him, "Pete, we're going to send you to a little village in Central Italy; you are going to live with a family there for eighteen months and all you've got to do is to learn to speak Italian."

Suppose at that moment any eighteen-month-old came tottering by and we told him to take the eighteen-month-old with him.

For the brilliant thirty-year-old, full instructions.

For the eighteen-month-old—no instructions.

Eighteen months later our brilliant thirty-year-old would speak a great deal of Italian—with a dreadful American accent.

The eighteen-month-old without instructions would also speak a great deal of Italian— with the precise accent of the house, of the village, of the province of Italy.

How do we explain that?

It's very simple.

All children are linguistic geniuses.

To a child born in Philadelphia tonight English is a foreign language. It is no more and no less foreign than German, Italian, Swahili or Urdu.

But by one year of age he understands a good deal and is beginning to say his first words.

By two years of age he understands a great deal and has a rudimentary ability to speak it.

By three years of age he understands and speaks it fluently enough to get by in almost all situations.

By six he speaks it perfectly to his own environment. If people in his neighborhood say, "I seen him when he done it," then so does he—but that's perfect to his environment.

If, on the other hand, his father is Professor of English at University College in London, then he speaks classical English with a classical English accent because that's perfect to his environment.

If he's born in a bilingual household where two languages are actually spoken, he speaks two languages.

If he's born into a trilingual language household where three languages are actually spoken, he speaks three languages—and so on, if not *ad infinitum,* at least as far as there are languages.

It is the greatest learning miracle I know of.

I first met Avi when he was nine years old in Rio, and at that time I could cheerfully have strangled him.

Avi spoke nine languages fluently.

What set me off was that he apologized for his English, which, he explained, he had learned mostly in school. He apologized for his English, in English, with a splendid B.B.C. accent. A B.B.C accent is better than an Oxford accent, which tends to be a bit mushy.

He apologized to me—me with my north Philadelphia accent. (A north Philadelphia accent is due mostly to a sinus condition as a result of the weather conditions).

If I am making an address to a scholarly group I can manage to sound reasonably scholarly, unless somebody makes me mad, in which case I'm right back to my north Philadelphia accent.

We had a President of the United States who said "Cuber" when he meant "Cuba."

The media teased him about it constantly but he kept on saying "Cuber." You can take the boy out of Boston but you can't take Boston out of the boy.

Avi had been born in Cairo in an English

speaking community; that gave him French, Arabic and English. His Spanish grandparents lived with them and that gave him Spanish. They moved to Haifa, (Yiddish, German and Hebrew) and his Turkish grandparents moved in with them, providing Turkish. Finally they moved to Brazil, which gave him Portuguese.

All the computers in the world hooked together could not carry on a free-flowing conversation at the thirty-month level in English, or French, or Arabic, or German, or Yiddish, or Turkish, or Hebrew, or Spanish, or Portuguese, never mind all of them and certainly not with a B.B.C. accent.

How then does this miracle beyond all miracles come about?

We fool ourselves into believing we taught them.

Rubbish.

Nobody would live long enough. There are 450,000 words in the English language and 100,000 in a first-rate vocabulary.

Nobody ever said to a two-year-old, "Look Johnny, these are called glasses." Instead we say, "Where are my glasses?"

"Give me my glasses."

"Don't pull off my glasses."

"My glasses need cleaning."

And Johnny, being a linguistic genius, says to

himself, "Those things are called glasses."

This ability, this incredible ability to learn a language (or ten) in the first three years is a miracle beyond comprehension which we take totally for granted.

It is a miracle which is observed as a miracle only in its absence.

When a tiny child does not learn to speak, then we instantly appreciate the size of the miracle in all its glory and complexity.

When that happens, parents from all over the world beg, borrow and steal to find the money necessary to beat their way to Philadelphia and the Institutes to say, "Tell us how to make the miracle happen."

A close friend of mine, a major of infantry, was stationed in Japan after World War II. He had been there a little more than a year when he heard some Japanese kids talking in the backyard. He looked out and one of them was his.

They were there for three years. When they came home, he and his wife had a Japanese vocabulary of eight words: *sayonara, konnichi-wa, arrigato, ohayo-gozaimasu* and so on.

Their Japanese friends couldn't understand their Japanese words, but their American friends could.

Cara Caputo, who had learned to speak

Japanese at the Institutes, went to visit a Japanese friend in Japan when she was just six years old. When she arrived, the Japanese school year was just beginning so Cara enrolled and went to school with her first grade Japanese friend. No problem of course.

It is easier to teach a one-year-old a foreign language than it is to teach a seven-year-old.

That's because *all* tiny children are linguistic geniuses.

9

birth to six

All that a baby is or may become will be determined in the first six years of life.

Nobody knows that better than tiny babies. They are in a hurry. As an example tiny kids want tools, not toys. No little kid ever invented a toy. Give a little boy a stick and it doesn't become a golf stick or a baseball bat, it becomes a hammer. Then of course he smashes his new hammer down on your lovely new cherry table to practice hammering. Back he goes to his rubber duck. Give a little girl a clam shell and it instantly becomes a dish, dirt and all.

What tiny children want is to be you. As soon as possible. They are right in so wanting.

The ability to take in raw facts is an inverse function of age.

You can teach a baby anything that you can present to him in an honest and factual way.

We have just seen the miracle of a child learning his native tongue—or four of them—with an ease that no adult can match.

As a young adult I spent night after night sitting up trying to learn French and I can't utter a single literate French sentence.

I spent not a single night as a child studying English but I learned to speak it without any help whatsoever and I write books that are read by millions of people.

Languages are made up of facts which are called words. Tens of thousands of them.

The ability to take in facts is an inverse function of age.

The older we get the harder it is to take in raw facts.

The younger one is the easier it is to take in raw facts.

It is easier to teach a five-year-old than it is to teach a six.

It is easier to teach a four-year-old than it is to teach a five.

It is easier to teach a three-year-old than it is to teach a four.

It is easier to teach a two-year-old than it is to teach a three.

It is easier to teach a one-year-old than it is to teach a two.

And, by George, it is easier to teach a six-month-old than it is to teach a one-year-old.

Ask yourself how many poems or rhymes you have learned during the last year and could now recite. The answer is probably few or none.

Now ask yourself how many rhymes you learned before you were six which you could still recite.

"Ring around a rosie..."

"London bridge is falling down..."

"Baa Baa black sheep..."

"My country tis of thee..."

"I pledge allegiance to the flag..."or whatever poem or jingles it was that people of your particular age learned as tiny children.

Ask yourself how many nights you sat up studying them. Or did you in fact learn them by some sort of tiny child osmosis?

The younger you are the easier it is to take in

facts—and keep them.

Most people believe that the older we get the brighter we get—not true.

The older we get the more wisdom we get. That's where adults have it all over kids, the older we get.

It must be obvious to you that we Institutes people hold children and parents in something approaching awe. That's true.

But we are in no way mystics. We haven't got a mystic bone in our collective body. We are intensely practical people who know about what works. But if we were going to be mystics it is certainly mothers and kids and the human brain about which we would be mystics.

But love, respect and admire kids as we do, we have never met a two-year-old with enough wisdom not to drown himself or to fall out of the fourth story window if adult vigilance slips for a minute.

Children do not have wisdom.

Infants are born with neither wisdom nor knowledge.

At birth, the ability to take in facts rises like the space shuttle taking off from the pad at Canaveral—almost straight up—and like that rocket, having reached a great height on a swiftly flattening curve, this ability quickly falls off to a line parallel to the ground.

By six the climb is virtually over.

The curve of wisdom, on the other hand, rises very slowly and by six it has really just come into being. It looks like this.

CURVES OF ABILITY AND WISDOM

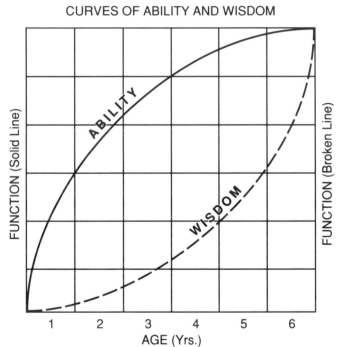

So the ability to learn rises like a rocket and then falls off quickly while wisdom rises slowly. At six years of age these lines meet.

At this point the child's ability to take in-formation without any effort whatsoever is just about gone for life, and significant brain growth is about done. He has become just about what he is going to be.

However, his wisdom is just beginning to develop. It will continue to grow through most of his life.

Just what and how much can he learn in those precious first six years?

Everything that matters.

It is easier to teach a one-year-old than it is to teach a seven-year-old.

Indeed it is *much* easier to teach a one-year-old.

Reading is nothing more than learning a large number of facts called words, and we have already seen that it is much easier to teach a one-year-old a new language through his ear than it is to teach a seven-year-old.

It is even easier to teach a baby a written language than it is to teach a spoken language. The written word is always the same. It doesn't have an accent, it is never slurred or spoken too softly.

The reader has already heard my confession about speaking French or understanding French through my ear. It's simple—I can't, not even a sentence. But I can read a French newspaper. I can also read a Portuguese news-paper. I don't get every word or phrase by a long shot—but I get the important thing. I get the message. I can easily read an Italian medical report or a Spanish one. I can read it at my own pace. I could not understand a French newspa-per being read to me, nor an Italian one. It's too fast and slurred; it won't stand still so I can figure it out. It is much easier to read a foreign word than it is to hear it.

To teach a one-year-old to understand a lan-guage through his ear there are only three re-quirements. The word must be loud, clear and repeated because the one-year-old's auditory pathway is immature.

All mothers have always instinctively and intu-itively spoken to their babies in a loud, clear voice and they have always said things repeated-ly. "COME TO MOMMY." "COME TO MOMMY," and the baby comes to Mommy.

In fact it is exactly the means by which the au-ditory pathway to the brain grows and matures.

That process is neurophysiological in nature.

The process of learning the message through the eye is also neurophysiological. Precisely the same process as the process of learning the message through the ear.

Again, there are three requirements. The message must be *large*, clear and repeated.

This, however, we have failed to do.

We have not shown babies words which are large, clear and repeated. In order to make a book or a newspaper light, cheap and easy to carry we have made the printing much too small for the immature visual pathways of the baby to see it.

This has had two results.

For ten thousand years we have kept written language a secret from babies, who are linguistic geniuses.

The visual pathways of our babies grow much more slowly than their auditory pathways.

The visual pathways, like the auditory pathways, *grow by use*.

Remember, the sensory pathways actually make up the entire back half of the brain.

We will discuss at greater length in a later chapter the importance of using a pathway so that it grows.

It is easier to teach a one-year-old to read than it is to teach a seven-year-old to read.

That is precisely why one-third of our seven- to seventeen-year-olds are failing to learn to read in school.

It is simply too late.

The miracle is not that one- third of them fail to learn to read in school—that's the problem.

The miracle is that two-thirds of them *do* learn to read at that late date.

Do you know that some medical schools are giving medical students remedial reading courses? If that doesn't scare you out of ten years' growth, I don't know what will.

And finally, although it is perhaps obvious, a good reason to teach a child to read *before* he goes to school is that he will not be among those unfortunate children who *fail* to learn to read once they get to school.

It is easier to teach a one-year-old to have encyclopedic knowledge than it is to teach a seven-year-old.

For all the same reasons we have just seen in reading it is also good for a child to have encyclopedic knowledge of a vast number of subjects.

This will greatly help him to be a great deal more educated when he goes to school.

It clearly makes him school-proof in much the same way that knowing how to swim well makes a child water-proof.

We shall tell you precisely how to give him encyclopedic knowledge in Chapter 18, "How to Give Your Baby Encyclopedic Knowledge."

It is easier to teach a one-year-old math than it is to teach a seven-year-old.

It is easier and better for all of the reasons already stated above.

Understanding mathematics when he goes to school also helps to make him school-proof. We shall teach you precisely how to teach your baby math (even if you can't do it) in Chapter 19, "How to Teach Your Baby Math."

If you teach your baby how to read, give him encyclopedic knowledge and teach him mathematics while he's a baby, you will give him

1. A love of mathematics which will continue to grow throughout his life;
2. An advantage in mastering related subjects;
3. Increased capability and intelligence;
4. Increased brain growth.

And, if this is not enough, he will also be a happier human being.

Children who are permitted to learn when learning is easiest don't spend much time being bored, or frustrated or causing upsets in order to get attention. They lead happier lives.

They like adults. They also like children. They make friends more easily and they keep those friends more easily than most children do.

Our children are easy to spot—they are the kids who are highly capable and highly confident and very, very gentle.

It is easier to teach a one-year-old any set of facts than it is to teach a seven-year-old.

Do you have a favorite subject that you can present to a baby in an honest and factual way? Go ahead. He'll learn it at a speed which will astonish you and he'll learn it superbly.

Do you love ornithology, art history, water skiing, Japanese, playing the guitar, reptiles, diving, ancient history, running, photography?

All you have to do is to figure out how to present it in an honest and factual way and by three he'll be an expert at it and he'll love it.

By twenty-one he'll be an authority on it or a champion in it if that's what he wants to be.

We encourage our children to be generalists and learn everything we can possibly offer them so they can do everything well.

Tiny kids learn facts at a tremendous rate which staggers the adult imagination.

Get him started and then step back.

If you teach a tiny kid the facts he will discover the rules that govern them.

It is a built-in function of the human brain.

To state it in a slightly different way: if you teach him the facts of a body of knowledge, he will discover the laws by which they operate.

A beautiful example of this exists in the mistakes that tiny children make in grammar. This apparent paradox was pointed out by the brilliant Russian author Kornei Chukovski in his book *From Two to Five* (University of California Press).

A three-year-old looks out a window and says, "Here comes the mailer."

"Who?" we ask.

"The mailer."

We look out the window and see the mailman. We chuckle at the childish mistake and tell the child that he is not called the mailer but the mailman.

We then dismiss the matter. Suppose that instead we asked ourselves the question, "Where did the child get the word mailer?" Surely no adult taught him the word "mailer." Then where did he get it?

I've been thinking about it for twenty-five years, and I am convinced that there is only one possibility.

The three-year-old must have reviewed the language to come to the conclusion that there are certain actions such as run, hug, kiss, sail, paint and that if you put the sound "*er*" on the end of them they become names and you have "runner," "hugger," "kisser," "sailor," "painter" and so on.

That's a whale of an accomplishment.

When did you last review a language to discover a law? May I suggest when you were three?

Still, we say it is a mistake because he is not the "mailer," he is the "mailman," and so the child is wrong.

Wrong word, yes, but right law.

The child was quite correct about the law of grammar he had discovered. The problem is that English is irregular and thus does not always follow logical rules. If it were regular the three-year-old would have been right.

Marvelous.

If you teach a tiny kid the laws he cannot as a result discover the facts.

We adults tend to divide all information into two kinds, which we call concrete and abstract. By concrete we mean what we understand and what is easily explained. By abstract we mean what we don't understand and what is therefore difficult if not impossible to explain.

Then we insist on teaching children abstractions.

The tiny child has a huge ability to discover the laws if we teach him the facts.

It is not possible to discover the facts, which are concrete, if we are taught only the rules, which are often abstractions.

The definition of science which appeals most to me is the one that says, "A branch of knowledge dealing with a body of facts systematically arranged to show the operation of laws."

That is a perfect explanation of how tiny kids approach all learning. First they absorb a huge number of facts, without the slightest effort, and then they arrange them systematically to discover the laws that govern them.

Tiny children use exactly the same method of solving problems as do scientists.

If I were forced to describe every genius that I have been privileged to know in a single word, the word I would use is curious.

I would dislike having to do so since all of the very brilliant people I have ever known are very different from each other. It is my chowderhead friends who are as alike as peas in a pod.

Scientists and geniuses are intensely curious.

Intense curiosity is a characteristic shared by true scientists, geniuses and all tiny children.

Tiny children *are* scientists.

Tiny children learn more fact for fact before-three years of age than they learn in the rest of their lives.

The Institutes' staff and, to our knowledge, one other group of people were saying that thirty years ago. Most people thought it to be silly.

Now everybody seems to be saying that.

It is true despite the fact that everybody says it.

Children could be learning *three times* as much during the first six years of life as they presently will learn in the rest of their lives.

Some children are, and what appealing children it makes them.

The word "learning" is not synonymous with the word "education."

Education begins at six—learning begins at birth.

Children are superb learners. They are limited only by how much material they have to learn about and how it is presented.

The first six years of life are the genesis of genius.

They are also the six years in which the brain

has most of its growth. Consider the miracle of head size.

At conception there is no head, just a single fertilized cell.

Nine months later the newborn baby has a head which is 35 centimeters in circumference.

By two and a half years it is 50 centimeters.

By twenty-one years it is 55 centimeters.

What a dramatic demonstration of brain growth and the very sharp way in which it drops off:

      9 months — 35 cm.
     21 months — 15 cm. more
    231 months — 5 cm. more

It is easy to make a baby a genius before six years of life.

And a great deal of fun for both baby and parents.

Sadly, it is extremely difficult to make a child a genius *after* six years of age.

The first six years of life are precious beyond measure.

10

what does I.Q.
really mean?

To answer the question which the title of this chapter poses we first have to determine how intelligence comes about.

We bring it about.

We've got six years of chronological time and then it's over.

Into those six years of elapsed or chronological time we can produce very little brain growth if that's what we want to produce.

All we need do is lock a baby in a closet and slip food under the door. If you lock him in a closet and give him no information for the first six years of his life, there's only one possibility: At age six he will be an idiot.

If, during the first six years of life, you don't lock him in a closet but treat him as if he were an idiot by ignoring him, he'll do a little better.

He'll be able to learn a bit on his own, he'll at least learn all there is to learn about his rubber duck, and he'll pick up English by listening to everybody around him talking. By the time he's six he'll be well below average six-year-olds and he'll have a true I.Q. of less than 100.

If you treat him exactly how average kids are treated he'll end up exactly average. In short, he will be intellectually six years old when he is six years old chronologically. That's what average means. He'll have an I.Q. of precisely 100.

If you understand the principles of how your child's brain grows you will deal with your child in a totally different manner during those vital first six years than you would otherwise have done.

This is so whether or not you ever pursue an organized and consistent program of reading, math or general knowledge.

If such were the case your child ought to arrive at six years of ability by the time he is four years old chronologically. That will give him an I.Q. of 150.

If you read this book and truly understand it and deal with him in a totally different way through all those vital six years of life and also teach him how to read and how to gain encyclopedic knowledge and how to do math, then he ought to have gained the six years of ability that an average six-year-old has no later than three years of age, and that will give him an I.Q. of 200 or above depending on how much before three years of age he reaches that all important sixth year of life.

What's even more important is that he will have the brain growth of a six-year-old by the time he is three years old. We will expand upon this all-important point in a later chapter.

When parents really understand this point it is often difficult for them to restrain themselves.

Frequently they find themselves saying to us, "Do you understand what you are *saying*? Do you realize how *important* it is?"

We do understand.

Indeed, we have been saying it for a very long time.

This is the very heart of why tiny children think that it is absolutely vital to grow up as quickly as possible.

There is a kind of neurological imperative within each child that demands it.

Don't you remember when you couldn't wait to be a teenager, and how desperately you wanted to be sixteen, and then to be eighteen, and then to be, at long last, twenty-one? And then twenty-one, and then twenty-one and then twenty-one?

All tiny kids want to grow up right now.

It is adults who want tiny children to stay tiny children. How often have you heard somebody say, "Wouldn't it be nice if they could just stay four years old forever?"

No parent of a brain-injured child ever said that.

They know the truth and it is their greatest fear that their four-year-old will stay four years old forever.

Nobody ever told the parent of a brain-injured child that we mustn't steal his precious childhood. Not unless he wanted a black eye. Those parents share a knowledge of the absolute truth. They share it with all little kids.

Certainly childhood is marvelous, providing you grow a day's worth every day. The problem with hurt kids is that they don't.

We have spent half a century finding ways to make hurt kids grow a day's worth every day.

When we found ways to make them grow *faster* than a day's worth everyday, we did it so they could catch up.

When some of them did catch up and kept right on going faster we found that to be remarkable.

In children who start out unhurt and therefore even with the board it's remarkable too. About twice the regular rate is very good—and faster is even better. The name of this book is *How to Multiply Your Baby's Intelligence* and that's what it means.

I.Q. means nothing more than this. It means how you compare with your peers. The rest is nonsense.

If a two-year-old can do everything that an average four-year-old can do and do it precisely as well, he's got an I.Q. of precisely 200.

No more and no less.

This is not based on some arbitrary and often ridiculous test he can pass but on what he can do.

Can you imagine what would have happened if Thomas Edison had been Thomas Edison three years sooner? Not three years added to the end of his life but to the beginning?

You couldn't get the same result by creating three Thomas Edisons. But then of course Thomas Edison *was* Thomas Edison three years sooner wasn't he? I mean he was a genius, wasn't he?

I don't know whether or not Thomas Edison

ever took an intelligence test in his life or not, but I know Leonardo didn't.

If we gave Linus Pauling an intelligence test and he got 100, would we take away his Nobel Prize?

Both of them?

Or would we conclude that it was the intelligence test which was wrong?

The only true test of intelligence is what a person does. Every minute of every day is an intelligence test and we all take that test every day.

Intelligence is not a theory, it's a reality.

Genius is as genius does.

No more and no less.

If ever there was a person who scored as a genius on an intelligence test but who never accomplished anything I would propose two things:

1. The world never heard of him;
2. The test doesn't measure intelligence.

Genius is as genius does.

The test of whether you can swim is swimming.

The test of whether you can play the violin is playing the violin.

The test of whether you can read is reading.

The test of whether you can speak Japanese is speaking Japanese.

The test of whether you are intelligent is whether you do intelligent things.

The test of whether you are a genius is whether you do genius things.

And nothing else.

The fact is that most highly intelligent people do get high scores on intelligence tests.

It does *not* mean that all people who get high scores on intelligence tests are highly intelligent.

Neither does it mean that people who do not score highly on intelligence tests are *not* highly intelligent.

It does mean that intelligence tests do not measure intelligence.

What you do in life measures intelligence—and genius.

Would you rather have a child who got a score of 150 on an I.Q. test and who didn't really do anything, or a child who could do everything and did so at age four instead of at age eight or perhaps not at all?

What children *can* do and *do*, in fact, *do* is the only true test of what they are.

That's what I.Q. *really* means.

11

on motivation
—and testing

One thing that scientists have discovered
is that often-praised children
become more intelligent
than often-blamed ones.
There's a creative element in praise.

—THOMAS DREIER

One of the most common questions we are asked is, "How can I motivate my child?"

That's two of our favorite questions. No we haven't made a mistake. We mean two questions. To truly answer that question we must deal with that marvelous things called motivation and its diametrical opposite—which is called testing, or dismotivation.

Let's go back to Matsumoto and Suzuki to see this beautifully illustrated.

The first question is, how have Prof. Suzuki and his people managed to select 100,000 splendid violin players at the age of two?

The answer is simple.

He hasn't.

These children have all been chosen by their mothers, each of whom has said simply, "I want my child to have the opportunity to play the violin."

The second question which is asked, interminably it seems, is, "How do you force a two-year-old to play the violin?"

The answer to that is also quite simple.

Nobody can force a two-year-old to do anything.

We adults, even those of us who love children dearly, constantly forget this, if we ever knew it.

Once in a while I see even our own splendid mothers make the mistake of trying to force their children to do something which they are not about to do.

It happens almost every day.

Mother and child are about to leave my office and mother says, "Bobby, say goodbye to Glenn Doman."

It has happened so often I can see it coming and I tense up.

There is a long silence.

Mother says, "Bobby, say goodbye to Glenn Doman."

There is another long silence.

I am very tense and now mother is tense.

Mother wishes she had never started this but now she feels obliged to see it through. Now through semi-clenched teeth she says, "Bobby! Say goodbye to Glenn Doman."

And nothing happens.

Now the tension in the office is so thick you could cut it with a knife.

Mother is as tense as she can be and so am I.

How about Bobby?

Bobby couldn't possibly be more relaxed. Bobby is quite simply tuned into a different station.

All little kids have in their heads a device very like those remote controls you use to change the channels on a television set. This device which all kids have is activated by a certain whining and demanding tone of the adult voice. The adult whines and whammo! He is on another channel. The adult voice doesn't go in one ear and out the other. It doesn't go in at all.

A brilliant father, sixty years ago, said that it is impossible to force the infant mind beyond that which brings it pleasure.

So all you must do to teach your little child anything is to arrange to bring him pleasure. And that doesn't mean play. Kids don't want to play, they want to learn.

So what do they do at Matsumoto?

They do exactly what we do, and have always done.

They arrange for the child to win.

How?

When a new mother and child arrive they are welcomed warmly by all of the "old" mothers and children.

Then the other children play the violin.

Now tell me—have you ever seen a two-year-old watching other two-year-olds with something in their hands who didn't say, "I want one of those things."?

In a very few days the new child is saying, "I must have one of whatever that thing is."

He is ready for his first lesson.

And what a first lesson it is.

If only every parent and school teacher alive could see that first lesson and understand it, the world would change overnight.

Picture in your mind this scene:

All the parents and children are seated in the auditorium. The new little child is about to get his first lesson.

Lying on a small table at the very front of the auditorium are a tiny violin and a tiny bow.

The child walks down the aisle toward the violin which he wants so much. He marches to the table and picks up the violin in one hand and the bow in the other. He then turns to face the audience—and he bows.

The audience applauds enthusiastically— and his first violin lesson is over.

You can almost hear him saying to himself, "Was *that* the first lesson? How soon do I get the *second* lesson? I wowed them in Matsumoto, wait till we get to Sheboygen."

They may not be the exact words in the mind of this little child but if you don't think that's the message he gets then you are in for some wonderful surprises when you start to teach your child.

Suzuki and his wonderful teachers have done exactly what we have always done.

They have arranged for the child to win.

It is exactly the opposite of what the school system does. Schools arrange for the child to lose.

It's called testing.

We shall have much to say about testing later in this book.

The purpose of testing is not, as the schools have always claimed, to determine what the child knows but rather to determine what he does *not* know.

All children love to learn and all children hate to be tested. In this respect they are exactly like all adults.

Everybody loves to learn and everybody hates to be tested. We like to test ourselves— privately.

So do little kids.

We have a 100 question spelling test and we get one word wrong. We get a big red X which shrieks, "No stupid! That isn't how you spell it."

The school system arranges for the child to lose—and sadly he frequently does.

Do I hear the strident voice of the Assistant Principal shouting, "But the purpose of testing is so that we can find out what the child doesn't know so that we can make sure that he learns it. We are really testing ourselves."

How about allowing the child to demonstrate what he does know?

The tragic truth is that it is much more efficient to discover what the child does not know and put a grade on it than it is to take the time and energy to allow the child to show his teachers what he does know.

And, of course, when he is found to be lacking, it is not his teacher who will face the ridicule of his peers; it is the child who will face the music.

Our job, whether we realize it or not, is to give our children a love for learning that will last for a lifetime. Since all children were born with a rage to learn, the least we can do is to not throttle it!

Are we against testing little children in school?

We are very much for testing in school *providing* that if the child does poorly, the child gets to criticize the teacher rather than the teacher criticizing the child.

We'd be very much in favor of testing children in school *providing* that if several children do poorly in a test, the teacher gets fired.

In that case the punishment would fit the crime.

Let's look at what Sir Winston Churchill said about testing and its opposite—motivation.

> *... I had scarcely passed my twelfth birthday when I entered the inhospitable regions of examinations, through which for the next seven years I was destined to journey. These examinations were a great trial to me. The subjects which were dearest to the examiners were almost invariably those I fancied least. I would have liked to have been examined in history, poetry and writing essays. The examiners on the other hand, were partial to Latin and mathematics. And their will prevailed. Moreover, the questions which they asked on both these subjects were almost invariably those to which I was unable to suggest a satisfactory answer. I should have liked to be asked*

> *to say what I knew. They always tried to ask what I did not know. When I would have willingly displayed my knowledge, they sought to expose my ignorance. This sort of treatment had only one result: I did not do well in examinations.*—My Early Life, Winston S. Churchill (Manor Books 1972).

Testing does not help a child to learn. Instead, a steady diet of testing slowly but surely eats away at the child's natural love of learning.

The teacher's job is to teach, not test.

The child's job is to learn.

Before we leave Matsumoto and Dr. Suzuki, let's summarize briefly and add a point.

What we and Dr. Suzuki do is arrange for the child to win. To win honestly of course, but to win.

Why is this important?

It is generally believed that success is a result of high motivation and that failure is a result of lack of motivation.

We have found that exactly the opposite is the case.

We propose that high motivation is a product of success and low motivation is a product of failure.

In many ways I am a childlike person. As an example, there are certain things in life which I do very poorly just as there are some things which I do rather well.

For instance I cannot carry a tune, which I would love to be able to do, and I cannot play tennis, which bothers me not at all.

I know that I should work hard on these two things in order to improve myself. I know I should. But I don't. I hate to admit it but to tell the whole truth, it's even worse. I tend to avoid them rather assiduously.

It's a dreadful confession but I feel better for having made it. I avoid like the plague those things which I do poorly.

On the other hand there are a few things I do pretty well. I find that when I do one of those things which I do well my friends congratulate me.

"Congratulations, Glenn, you did that splendidly."

"Yes, that wasn't bad was it? Would you like to see me do it again?"

There you have it. Those things I do badly I avoid doing. Those things I do well I tend to do over and over again.

Little kids are just like me.

The lesson is simple.

If you want your baby to dislike something be sure to point out all the ways in which what he did fell short of perfection.

If you want to see him love to do something (and do it over again and again to show you how well he does it) then tell him all the things that were splendid about what he did.

If you want to destroy his motivation altogether just keep testing him and pointing out how far he is from perfect.

If you want to increase his motivation find out everything that he is doing right and tell him about it enthusiastically.

Although Winston Churchill did not do well in examinations at school he did exceedingly well in the test of real life.

Surely he was one of the greatest geniuses in the art of motivation of this century.

He never lied to the British people. He told them the absolute truth (just as we never lie to children).

In those darkest days of World War II he told them:

"I have nothing to offer you but blood, sweat and tears."

"Let us so conduct ourselves, that if the British Empire should endure for a thousand years, men will say, 'This was their finest hour.'"

He didn't tell the British how poor they were but rather how great they were and how much greater they would become.

The American broadcaster Edward R.

Murrow said of Churchill:

"He marshalled the English language—and hurled it into battle."

Indeed he did; it was about all he had to hurl.

Telling the British people how great they were proved to be enough.

Tell your kid how great he is and how much you love him.

Tell him often.

Even if it is all you have to give him—it will be enough.

12

the brain–
use it or lose it

It is said that familiarity breeds contempt. That saying is half true. It is true if the person, thing or knowledge with which one becomes familiar is contemptible.

It is certainly not true about the human brain, at least in the long love affair which we have been carrying on with the human brain.

The staff stands in awe of the human brain and it is a love affair which we hope to share with you.

Try this if you wish to begin sharing our awe. If you happen to be pregnant right now, look at your watch and, starting now, count out exactly sixty seconds.

During that one minute, your unborn baby gained approximately a quarter of a million new brain cells. How does that strike you?

It is vital to remember that when we speak of the human brain, we are speaking of that physical organ which occupies the human skull and the spinal column, and which weighs three-and-a-half to four pounds.

We are not speaking of the nebulous thing called the "mind," which is talked about *ad infinitum* and often *ad nauseum* and is the province of the psychiatrist and the psychologist.

While it is talked about endlessly, not a great deal is known about it, and much of that is fiddle-faddle and has of late been called "psychobabble."

It is the confusion between the much-discussed, and little-understood "mind" and that physical organ called "the brain" about which much has been known which has caused the problem.

The Incas, Greeks, and Egyptians practiced successful brain surgery. Hippocrates himself performed successful brain surgery 2,400 years ago.

We deal with the brain.

The conventional wisdom is that very little is known about that mysterious organ the human brain beyond the fact that it weighs three or four pounds and that it is responsible in some way for walking, talking and to some degree for thinking. This same convention asserts that the only thing that is well known is that it is not capable of being changed.

As is so often the case, the truth is much better than the fiction.

The human brain is an organ superb beyond anyone's imagining.

Much has been known about it for many thousands of years. Of all the organs of the human body it is the most capable of change in both directions.

It is, in point of fact, constantly changing in a physical as well as a functional way, either for better or for worse.

In a very small number of people the improvements are being made purposefully, and effectively. In the vast majority of us the brain is being wasted accidentally.

If what the fiction intends to propose is that much remains to be learned about the human brain, that is probably true.

What the fiction actually says is that little is known about it. In an anatomical, physiological and functional sense, such a view is nonsense.

We can see it, hear it, feel it and touch it in the operating room. Most important is the fact that we can influence it (favorably or unfavorably). We can stop its growth, we can slow its growth and we can speed its growth.

The human brain contains more than a trillion (1,000,000,000,000) cells.

The human brain contains more than ten billion functioning neurons (10,000,000,000) at a very conservative estimate.

We presently use a very small percentage of these ten billion neurons.

There are many single statements in this book which, if they are truly understood by the reader along with their application to the child, are worth the price of the book and the time required to read it a hundred times over. One of those statements is: *Function determines structure.*

The fact that function determines structure is a well-known law of architecture, engineering and human growth, although in the sense of its application to human growth little attention has been paid to it.

That function determines structure is seen most clearly in architecture.

If one said to an architect, "I would like you to build me a building with a floor space of 1600 square feet," the first question the architect would ask is, "What is the building going to be? Will it be a house, an office, a grocery store, a garage, or what?"

If he is to build a sensible building, he must know what it is for, because its function will determine its structure.

This is also true in terms of the human body. The case of the human being who is a weight-lifter shows this clearly. His muscles and body grow in exact relationship to his weight lifting and thus his function, weight lifting, has determined his structure (extraordinarily muscular).

The person who does an average amount of physical activity has average muscular development. The person who does a very small amount of physical exercise has a very small amount of muscular development.

It is also true that lack of function produces a poor structure.

While we already know that generally body structure (tall, short, broad, narrow) is essentially a genetic familial inheritance, even that can be grossly altered by lack of function.

This happens far too often when insane parents chain an infant to a bed post in an attic or lock a baby in a closet. Tragically, this occurs over and over again through the ages and in almost every nation. The result is, of course, tragic and is the ultimate in child abuse, comparable only to killing the child.

A recent case in the United States was revealed when a nine-year-old girl who had been kept in a closet was discovered.

Her body was the size of a two-and-a-half year-old child and her brain development was virtually nil. She was, of course, speechless and an idiot. She could have been nothing else. So too would Leonardo, Shakespeare, Edison or Pauling have been, under the same circumstances.

Brain-injury, which by its nature prevents function to a slight or to an almost total degree depending upon its severity and its location, results in smaller bodies.

In this case it is the brain-injury, rather than the environment (the closet), which prevents function.

The vast majority of severely brain-injured children are quite tiny when they are first seen at the Institutes. That is to say, in height, in chest, in head size, in weight, they are, in 78 per cent of the cases, significantly below average, and 51 per cent are among the smallest 10 per cent of the population, sometimes very small even in that group.

Yet at birth (except for the premature ones) they tended to be at or very near average size. As they get older they become smaller and smaller compared to children their own age, since the lack of physical functioning results in a lack of physical structure.

This is exactly the opposite of what happens to the weight lifter.

Yet once we start such a child on a program of child brain development, his rate of growth will change, and often change dramatically.

Quite often a child who had been growing far more slowly than normal will suddenly start to grow far faster than normal for his age. Even where he began the program smaller in height, in head and chest circumference and in weight than 90 per cent of other children in his age bracket, it is commonplace to find him suddenly growing at 250 per cent of the norm for his age.

While this phenomenon appears to be virtually unknown to those dealing with brain-injured children, it is well known to anthropologists and even has a name. It is called the catch-up phenomenon.

This rule says that if a child is seriously ill for any reason, his physical growth will slow down or virtually stop, depending on the illness and its severity. The rule further states that if the child becomes well for any reason, he will then grow faster than his peers to catch up. This, of course, is why it is called the catch-up phenomenon.

We see this occurring every day of our lives at the Institutes.

We see also, and it is hardly surprising, that there seems to be a high correspondence between the rate of success and the rate of growth as well as between the ultimate degree of growth and the ultimate degree of success.

That is to say, children who fail to make progress also fail to change in growth rate, children who succeed markedly but not completely, grow markedly but not completely, and children who succeed entirely, grow entirely.

While this rule, like all other rules I know, is not invariable, it is almost always so.

This is simply another way of saying that lack of function creates an immature or abnormal structure and that normal function determines normal structure.

At the Institutes, all brain-injured children (except those who are completely blind) are started on a program of reading words, using extra-large print so that the words can be discerned by the immature visual pathways.

When blind children come to the Institutes the first step is to give them the ability to see outline. When this is accomplished a reading program is begun.

There are, as a result, many hundreds of brain-injured children two, three or four years old, who can read with total understanding—from a few words for some, to many, many books for others.

We know many brain-injured three-year-olds who can read in several languages with complete understanding.

Although the world at large believes that children under five are unable to read because their visual pathways are too immature and because their brains are not sufficiently developed, there are hundreds of two-, three- and four-year-olds who are in fact reading.

What is more, they are brain-injured and what is more, their visual pathways are now more highly developed than are the visual pathways of older children who are not brain-injured and who do not read.

How can this possibly be explained?

It certainly cannot be explained on the basis of age, since they are younger, not older, than the well six-year-olds who have not yet been taught to read.

It certainly cannot be explained on the grounds of some natural superiority. Far from being superior, these children are brain-injured and have often previously been diagnosed as being mentally retarded.

I don't know anyone who believes it is an advantage to be brain-injured.

It can be explained only on the grounds that these children have simply had an opportunity to read that other children have not had. That opportunity permitted function, and function in turn created more mature visual pathways, since function determines structure.

We see then that since function determines structure, the child's body grows by use, or fails to grow as a product of disuse.

But the visual pathways are in the brain and are part of the brain itself.

What does that mean?

The brain grows by use.

This principle is the single most important principle of child brain development.

How can we know that the brain physically grows by use?

We have already seen how the child who is unable to function as a result of being confined, grows almost not at all.

We have also seen how the brain-injured child whose function is markedly reduced grows at a much slower rate physically but who, when made able to function, grows at an above average rate to catch up.

We have also seen how his head size grows at an increased rate in order to catch up. The skull grows in order to accommodate the brain which has grown larger.

This demonstrates that the brain grows by use.

I have *rarely* met a human being concerned with children who was aware of this all-important fact. In fairness, I must report that when such people learn that this is so, they are almost universally both delighted and excited.

On the other hand, I have *never* met a neurophysiologist who did *not* know that the brain grows by use.

The problem is that neurophysiologists rarely deal with children or with the people who do deal with children.

Neurophysiologists deal almost exclusively with rats, kittens, puppies, monkeys and other animals.

Now let's look at animal experimentation.

First, there is the work of the brilliant neurosurgeon and neurophysiologist, Boris N. Klosovskii, who was Chief of Neurosurgery at the Academy of Medical Sciences of the U.S.S.R.

Dr. Klosovskii had taken litters of newborn kittens and puppies and had divided them into two equal groups, one as the experimental group and the other as the control group.

Into the experimental group he had placed a female kitten and into the control group he had placed a sister from the same litter. He then did the same thing with each of the male kittens from each litter and he divided the puppies in the same fashion until he had two perfectly matched groups, each containing kittens and puppies from each of the litters.

The kittens and puppies in the control group were then permitted to grow in the usual way in which kittens and puppies normally grow.

The experimental animals, however, were simply placed on a slowly revolving turntable and lived there throughout the experiment.

The turntable was rather like the revolving restaurants one sees on tops of towers in large cities. Obviously they turn very slowly, lest the diner lose his cookies.

The only difference, then, in what had happened to each of the groups was that the experimental group saw a moving world while the control group saw only as much as newborn kittens and puppies normally see.

When the animals were ten days old, Klosovskii began to sacrifice matched pairs of the kittens and puppies and to take their brains. He had sacrificed the last of them by the nineteenth day of life.

What Klosovskii found in the brains of his experimental animals should be required reading for every parent of a small child.

The experimental animals had from 22.8 to 35.0 percent more growth in vestibular areas of the brain than did the control animals.

To state the same thing in plain language, in ten to nineteen days of seeing a moving world, the experimental kittens and puppies had almost one third more brain growth in balance areas of the brain than did their brothers and sisters who had not seen a moving world.

This is more astonishing when one considers that a ten-day-old kitten or puppy (or even a nineteen-day-old kitten or puppy) is not yet much of a kitten or a puppy. Even so, the animals that saw a moving world had almost one-third more brain growth (and some of them more than one-third more).

Just what does more growth mean? Did Klosovskii see one-third larger numbers of brain cells in his microscope? Not at all; he saw the same number of brain cells, but one third larger and one third more mature.

When I consider the control animals, I think of average three- and four-year-old children, and when I think of the experimental kittens and puppies with one-third more brain growth, I think of our hurt kids who are reading. Then

I cannot help wondering what would have happened if Klosovskii had taken a third group of kittens and puppies and put them in near darkness. Would they have had one-third less brain growth? This is virtually what happens to little Xingu babies, who live in dark huts in Brazil's Mato Grosso for about their first year of life.

But Klosovskii did not have a third group of animals, and thus we cannot know how it would have been.

Perhaps, however, we can deduce what might have happened had Klosovskii had a third group by going to the opposite end of the world to meet that genius David Krech, whose team's brilliant work at Berkeley supplies us with our second example.

Dr. Krech was not only a scientist with great scientific knowledge whose impeccable conclusions are beyond question, he also had great wisdom.

This is a wonderful combination because science is not always wise, nor is all wisdom scientific. How I wish that gentle, witty David Krech could be heard by all parents rather than only by those who read scientific journals.

Dr. Krech had spent an important portion of his life repeating an experiment with slight modifications each time. He began by raising two sets of infant rats. One set lived in an environment of sensory deprivation; that is to say, an environment in which there was little to see, hear or feel. The other rats were raised in an environment of sensory enrichment; that is to say, one in which there was a great deal to see and hear and feel.

He then tested the intelligence of the rats by such tests as putting food in mazes. The deprived rats either could not find the food or found it with great difficulty. The rats raised in the enriched environment found the food easily and quickly.

He then sacrificed the rats and examined their brains.

"Rats which have been raised in sensory deprivation," he noted, "have small, stupid, underdeveloped brains, while rats which have been raised in sensory enrichment have large, intelligent, highly developed brains."

He then stated his scientific conclusion which, befitting a world-famous neurophysiologist, was scientifically immaculate.

"It would be scientifically unjustifiable," said Dr. Krech, "to conclude that because this is true in rats that it is also true in people."

Then he added great wisdom.

"And it would be socially criminal to conclude that it is not true in people."

The last time I had the opportunity to see Dr. Krech, I asked him if he envisioned doing anything about people.

His eyes twinkled as he replied, "I have not devoted my life to this for the purpose of creating more intelligent rats."

What is the advantage of having the brain grow by use and thus have larger and more mature cells? It is precisely the same advantage in an intellectual sense that the Olympic gymnast Nadia Comaneci had in a physical sense when she did those superb gymnastic feats with such grace and beauty.

What is more, the more she did them, the more her muscles and coordination grew, and the more this happens the more graceful and beautiful became her movements.

Because physical movements such as Nadia's are controlled entirely by the brain, the more beautifully and successfully she did these things the more her brain grew and the higher her mobility intelligence was able to rise. She was obviously a mobility genius.

In the same way a child's visual intelligence and auditory intelligence rises sharply when he has the opportunity to learn a huge number of facts at a very young age. Whether these facts be in the form of encyclopedic types of facts, facts in the form of words or facts in the form of numbers, his intelligence will rise in proportion to the number of facts he is given.

What is more, his brain will grow physically as a result.

Perhaps most important of all, is that since the one-, two-, or three-year-old would rather learn than do anything else in the world, both he and his mother will have a delightful time in the process.

By its nature, the process of a mother teaching a baby in an honest and factual way is a mutually loving and respectful process, and it grows the brain.

All significant brain growth is finished by six years of age.

Nature has superbly planned her most astonishing invention, the human brain, so that in those all-important first six years of life it can take in facts at lightning speed. The child will have this vast storehouse of information (we shall shortly see just how vast that storehouse is) to last a lifetime. Those facts will be the basis upon which knowledge and wisdom will grow and prosper.

What we do not use, we lose.

The fact that what we do not use, we lose is so well known that it is almost axiomatic in everything from biceps to algebra and needs no further amplification here.

The knowledge that the brain grows by use during the first six years of life and that we can grow the child's brain almost at will is not valuable, it is *invaluable*.

The entire back half of the brain and spinal cord (the spinal cord is the ancient brain and parent to the pons, midbrain and cortex) is made up entirely of the five incoming sensory pathways.

We can literally grow it by giving the child visual, auditory, tactile, olfactory and gustatory information with increased frequency, intensity and duration. They are the pathways by which we gain all information. Use them and they will grow and become more mature and competent. Fail to use them during those six years and they will not.

The front half of the brain and spinal cord is composed of the outgoing motor pathways by which we respond to that incoming sensory information.

These pathways in human beings result in mobility competence, language competence and manual competence. These pathways also grow by use.

These two sets of pathways *are* the brain. They grow physically bigger and more competent by use.

It is not true that we use only a tenth of our

brain. We do not live long enough to use a thousandth of our brain's potential.

Perhaps Leonardo may have come close to using a thousandth of his brain's potential— that's why he was Leonardo.

The human brain has a capacity of one hundred and twenty-five trillion, five hundred billion (125,500,000,000,000) bits of information.

While the staff of the Institutes has long been aware that the capacity of the human brain was vast, almost beyond belief, it was not until scientists at the R.C.A. Corporation Advanced Technical Laboratories issued the following chart that the full extent of that capacity was comprehended.

HOW MEMORY CAPACITIES COMPARE

Memory Device	Storage Capacity (millions of characters)
Human brain	125,500,000
National Archives	12,500,000
IBM 3850 magnetic cartridge	250,000
Encyclopaedia Britannica	12,500
Optical disc memory	12,500
Magnetic (hard) disc	313
Floppy disc	2.5
Book	1.3

Source: RCA Corp. Advanced Technology Laboratories

Ten times the capacity of the national archives of the United States of America:

The four pound human brain.

Do you begin to join us in our awe of the human brain?

If your baby had only a *tenth* of his brain capacity he would be reduced to the capacity of the national archives.

Still worried about using it up?

Or are you worried that it will go to waste?

The human brain is the only container which has the characteristic that the more you put into it, the more it will hold.

It is clear that no human being in history has ever come close to using it up. It is also clear that it grows by use and therefore the more information you put into it the better it can perform, and the more cross references it can make with that information.

When you improve one function of the brain you improve all functions of the brain to some degree.

There are six functions of the human brain which set all humans apart from other creatures. They are all unique to humans because they are all functions of the unique human cortex. Only humans have these six functions. Three of them are motor functions and three of them are sensory functions.

1. Only humans walk in a totally upright position using their arms and legs in a cross-pattern of movement;
2. Only humans talk in a contrived, abstract, symbolic, conventional language;
3. Only humans oppose thumb to finger and with a pencil or by other means write that language which they have invented.

These three uniquely human motor functions are based on three uniquely human sensory skills.

1. Only humans see in such a way as to be able to read that written language they have invented;
2. Only humans hear in such a way as to understand that spoken language through their ears;
3. Only humans feel in such a way as to identify an object by touch alone.

These six things are the test of Humanity.

Competence in these six things is the neurological test of normality.

These six things are the school's test of normality.

These six things are society's test of normality:
Mobility Intelligence

Language Intelligence
Manual Intelligence
Visual Intelligence
Auditory Intelligence
Tactile Intelligence.

An individual child or adult who does these six things below his peers is below average.

An individual who does these six things on an absolute par with his peers is called average.

An individual who does these six things above his peers is above average to the degree that he does these things above his peers.

Intelligence is the result of thinking.

For too long the world has had the notion that thinking is the result of intelligence. Which came first, the chicken or the egg?

Does it matter which came first?

It makes a whale of a difference.

If humans as a group, or a human as an individual, is simply assigned an individual predestined intelligence then it doesn't make a lot of difference. But this is not so.

If Einstein or you had been confined in a closet at birth and kept there for thirteen years he would have been an idiot and you wouldn't be reading this book.

Humans, at birth, are assigned the potential intelligence of *Homo sapiens,* and that is vast beyond measure. It is clear that humans use as much of that virtually unlimited potential as they are permitted to use by accidental circumstance, either good or bad.

If he is not permitted to think by having no facts or information to think about he will develop no intelligence.

We may therefore conclude that intelligence is the result of thinking.

Humans are intelligent because they use their brains.

Our children's brains grow as much as we give them the opportunity to grow.

We give them this opportunity by presenting them with a huge number of clear facts. We do this prior to six years of age, during which time they can learn them at a startling rate. Further, we do this when the brain is growing faster than it ever will again.

These facts take the form of words, numbers and encyclopedic information, which quickly move to sentences, mathematical computations and laws of nature and humanity.

Our children are as intelligent as we give them the opportunity to be.

This is most especially true during the first six years of life.

Intelligence is entirely a product of the human brain.

Human intelligence is most particularly a

product of the human cortex. Only humans have a human cortex and only humans need one.

13

mothers make the very best mothers—and so do fathers

God could not be everywhere and therefore he made mothers.

—JEWISH PROVERB

Mothering, and not the other one, is the oldest profession.

It just has to be, doesn't it?

And a most honorable and ancient profession it is.

Perhaps that's the reason mothers, along with children and geniuses, have such a bad press. Perhaps we are just a bit intimidated by them.

The myths about mothers outnumber the myths about geniuses and kids.

They are so ridiculous that they would be high humor if the results of the myths weren't so dreadful.

The greatest myth about mothers is that they cannot be trusted either to know or to understand their own children because they are too emotionally involved with them.

Only "professional" people are capable of knowing or understanding children.

If this be so then surely the lives of our children are far too important to be left in the hands of their mothers.

Well that's the myth.

The reality is that mothers know more about children than anyone alive, and until about two hundred years ago they were the *only* people who knew anything about children.

Mothers, without the help of a single teacher, child psychologist, child psychiatrist, obstetrician, pediatrician or reading expert had managed to get us from the Pleistocene caves of prehistoric man up to what has been very properly called the "Age of Reason".

We professionals, who had our own beginning in the "Age of Reason" and who began to take over children about that time, have managed to take us (virtually overnight as geologists measure time) from the "Age of Reason" to the "Atomic Age."

We should all ponder that questionable bit of progress.

The problem is that most professionals simply do not trust parents to deal with children.

Among professional people who deal with mothers and children there is an untaught and unspoken law which says, "All mothers are idiots and they have no truth in them."

No one ever really *says* it but it's a law all right.

The closest one ever comes to hearing it is the oft-repeated statement, "The raising of children is too important to be left to mothers."

The truth is that the raising of children is too important to be left to anyone *other* than mothers and fathers.

Indeed it is mothers themselves who have taught me the absolute truth, which is that mothers know more about their own children than anyone else in the world.

It took living with mothers by the thousands to teach me that truth.

Myths are powerful indeed.

Among those thousands of superb mothers we have met some lazy, crazy and selfish mothers. It is just that we have met far fewer lazy, crazy, selfish mothers than the number of lazy, crazy, selfish members in any other group of people we have known. It seems fair to add that we have been privileged to know some magnificent groups of people.

The problem is that mothers have been bullied so long by professional people that they are in danger of being bullied out of their superb instinctual and intuitive behavior with their own children.

Mother reads an article in a ladies' magazine by a Ph.D. (very often a *male* Ph.D.) which says, in effect, "Spare the rod and spoil the child." It continues to say that a stern hand is required at the tiller and there's nothing like a good old-fashioned spanking administered regularly and heavily to keep the kids in line.

Mother says to herself, "That doesn't sound right to me but I'm only a mother and he's a Ph.D."

I'm only a mother. Only a mother?

Mother doesn't really take up spanking her child as a regular practice but it does worry her.

A short time later she reads another article in another ladies' magazine by another Ph.D. (this one a bachelor). Problem is, this one's saying, "Never, never, never put a finger on your child or you'll ruin his little psyche and he'll grow up to hate your gaudy guts."

Now what the devil is mother to do?

She's got conflicting orders from two different people and they're both Ph.D.'s.

And what's more they are both from famous universities or at least state teachers' colleges.

Mother says to herself, "That doesn't sound right either but what to do? I'm only a mother."

Only a mother?

There is an old Spanish proverb that says, "An ounce of mother is worth a pound of clergy."

Or a babble of academics.

So what is mother to do?

Fair question. I don't really know. But I have an overwhelming suspicion that if all mothers could forget all advice from all professionals (including the ones who wrote this book) every time this particular question arose and took the following action, that it would almost always work out well.

If every time mother had a strong feeling that she ought to hang one on her child's rear-end, no matter what anybody said, she did so, and, that if every time she had a strong feeling that she should pick him up in her arms and love him, no matter what anybody said, she did so, I think she'd be right 99% of the time and I don't know any professional, including this one, who's right 99% of the time about anything.

Mothers are not the problem for children—mothers are the answer.

It is professionals who believe mothers are

the problem, and in this, at least, professionals are wrong.

Let's consider the most basic of the myths: the problem with mothers is that they are emotionally involved with their children.

Surely this implies that somehow children would be better off if their mothers were *not* emotionally involved with them.

Stop for a moment and imagine a world in which mothers were not emotionally involved with their children.

What kind of a world would it be?

Even Napoleon once stopped invading long enough to say, "Let France have good mothers, and she will have good sons."

Even Wellington would have agreed with that.

The myth about emotional involvement goes on to say that because mothers are emotionally involved with their kids they can't be objective about them.

It gets funnier—and sadder.

The clearest and most common example quoted of this lack of objectivity is the claim that each mother secretly thinks her own tiny child is a genius, and if that doesn't prove that mothers can't be objective about their own babies, what does?

Buckminster Fuller said, "Every wellborn child is originally geniused, but is swiftly degeniused by unwitting humans and/or physically unfavorable environmental factors."

It is said that it takes one to know one and I guess that, at least in this case, it applies to geniuses.

Every young mother looks at her baby and sees exactly what that genius Buckminster Fuller saw. Since no one ever told her that all babies are born "geniused" she can only conclude that her only her baby is a genius.

She's right of course—her baby is a genius.

The only mistake she makes is in saying it. Once she makes the observation that her baby is extremely bright she proves that she is incapable of being objective about him.

It's of more than passing interest to know that many, many geniuses have noted that babies are geniuses. We could easily have filled this chapter with such quotations.

Geniuses look at babies—and see themselves.

Mothers see the same things in babies that geniuses see. The only thing is mothers are not allowed to say it—geniuses are.

Although the myths about mothers go on and on we shall restrict ourselves to only one more: mothers are very competitive and wish their children to be better than other children.

Despite constant accusations that mothers are highly competitive in things related to their children, and wish devoutly that their own children would outstrip all the kids in the neighborhood in physical, intellectual and all other terms, we have not found this to be the case in the vast majority of the mothers with whom we have been privileged to work.

What we find mothers want is not that their children be better than everyone else but simply that they be as effective as they are capable of being. Mothers the world over are virtually positive that such is not presently the case.

As usual—they're right.

The process of learning is a joyous one for both mother and child.

Mothers and kids are the most dynamic and exciting learning combination possible and have always been since mothers started that process a long time ago.

Not only is this so but it's a wonderful thing for mothers themselves. We learned this a long time ago.

I am reminded of how astonishingly far we have come since May of 1963 when the Gentle Revolution began so quietly with the publication of our article, "Teach Your Baby To Read," in *Ladies' Home Journal.*

That article was published about the same time the phenomenon which came to be called "Women's Lib" began to emerge.

Many changes have taken place in our society as a result of both these events.

One of the most important and least noticed of the results of these two developments is that each has had a fascinating and beguiling effect on the other.

As women began to seek, demand and find their proper place in the sun of world affairs, there arose women congressmen, women governors, women astronauts and women leaders in all forms of government, religion, science, industry, law and all other walks of life. Simultaneously another kind of women's leadership was ever so quietly taking place. Of all the changes it was the most widespread, the most pervasive, the most powerful and the least heralded.

Millions of young women watched other women moving into what had been men's jobs and professions.

However they found that they wanted a different sort of profession and a very different sort of life for themselves. They discovered that they wished to be what we have chosen to call "professional mothers."

It was not so much that they didn't want to enter the male world. It was that they wanted much more to be mothers.

They did not accept the modern myth of

motherhood as a kind of slavery in which women were supposedly sacrificed to a humdrum life of dirty diapers and house cleaning.

These women saw motherhood as the most exciting and rewarding profession they could imagine.

They were no less concerned than other women about the state of the world and about changing it for the better.

They believed that they had a vital role to play in changing the world and making it a better place.

They had decided that the best way to change the world for the better was not by improving the world's institutions, but by improving the world's people. They controlled the world's most important resource and raw material—babies.

Mothers were deeply concerned about the collapse of the school system so evident on every hand.

Mothers, quietly, and in ever-increasing numbers, decided simply to take matters into their own hands. Their husbands, in ever-increasing numbers quietly agreed. Neither the school systems, the parent-teacher associations, the school boards nor the action committees seemed able to do more than stem the tide of ever more expensive and ever less productive schooling.

They decided that they would be professional mothers.

And it was about this time that their gentle revolution discovered the other Gentle Revolution.

The results have been truly incredible.

When this new kind of mother discovered that she could not only teach her baby to read, but teach him better and easier at two years of age than the school system was doing at seven, she got the bit firmly between her teeth—and a new and delightful world opened up.

A world of mothers, fathers and children.

It has within it the potential to change the world in a very short time and almost infinitely for the better.

Young, bright and eager mothers taught their babies to read in English and sometimes in two or three other languages.

They taught their children to do math at a rate that left them in delighted disbelief.

They taught their one-, two- and three-year-olds to absorb encyclopedic knowledge of birds, flowers, insects, trees, presidents, flags, nations, geography and a host of other things.

They taught them to do gymnastic routines on balance beams, to swim and to play the violin.

In short they found that they could teach their tiny children absolutely anything which they could present to them in an honest and factual way.

Most interesting of all, they found that by doing so, they had multiplied their babies' intelligence.

Most important of all, they found that doing so was, for them and for their babies, the most delightful experience they had ever enjoyed together.

Their love for each other and perhaps even more important, their respect for each other, multiplied.

How were these mothers different from the mothers who had always been?

Not only is it true that mothering was the oldest profession but it is also true that mothers were the first teachers and they remain *the best* teachers who have ever existed.

It was mothers, after all, who have brought us from the caves of *Australopithecus* to the Age of Reason.

One wonders if we professionals, who brought us from the Age of Reason to the Atomic Age are going to take the world as far in the next hundred thousand years as the mothers have brought us in the last.

How then were our new professional mothers different from the mothers who had always been?

They were different in two ways. My own mother seems to me to be typical. She raised her children, of whom I am the eldest, with profound love and an intuitive balance of just the right mixture of parental spoiling and parental discipline. She did so, however, at great personal sacrifice and had found her sole reward in vicarious appreciation of our personal progress.

To those ancient virtues and intuitions our professional mothers had added two new dimensions. Those dimensions were professional knowledge added to ancient intuition, and taking their pleasure now, in the doing, added to the vicarious pleasures to come later.

No drudgery here among these young mothers. To be sure they have still to deal with dirty diapers and household chores as had my own mother. But no longer do they face a lifetime which has only such chores to offer.

Not by a long shot.

These mothers are having a second education which is proving to be much more fruitful and rewarding to their own growth and development than they had ever imagined.

At a time of life which had been my mother's peak, their life is, in a very real sense, just beginning.

The Institutes does not actually teach children at all. It really teaches mothers to teach their children. Here, then, are our young mothers, at the prime of life, not at the beginning of the end, but rather at the end of the beginning.

They are themselves, at 25 or at 32, learning to speak Japanese, to read Spanish, to play the violin, to do gymnastics; and they attend concerts, visit museums, and a host of other splendid things which most of us dream of doing at some dim time in the distant future (which for most of us never comes). The fact that they are doing these activities with their own tiny children multiplies their joy in doing them.

They experience a sense of high purpose and take pride in their children and the contributions those children will make to the world.

They also have expanded and increased their own knowledge and find that they are more confident and more capable than they were before they began to teach their children.

They expected their children to change but they are astonished to discover that they themselves have higher expectations and bigger goals for their lives as a result of being professional mothers.

Nice side effect, isn't it?

These are professional mothers.

Does it mean that unless a mother is willing to be a full-time professional mother it is impossible for her to multiply her baby's intelligence?

Of course not.

The thousands of mothers (and fathers) whom we know fall generally into three groups.

The first group are the full-time mothers we have just described. They approach their career as a mother with the same dedication and professionalism that any other serious professional does. They are absolutely devoted to their babies.

The second group are the mothers who spend a great deal of time with their babies but not full time. They also are absolutely devoted to their babies. Their reasons for devoting less than full time range from economic necessity to having a great desire to do additional things.

The third group of mothers we see are those who can spend only short periods of time with their babies. They also are absolutely devoted to their babies. The majority of this group of mothers are forced by dire financial need to spend a major part of their time outside their home.

This is tragic for these mothers and for their babies.

A sane society should provide a way for every mother who *wants* to be home with her child to be home with that child.

All of these groups of mothers share the characteristic that they are completely devoted to their babies and as a consequence are determined that their babies will have the opportunity to be everything good that it is possible for them to be in life.

Obviously there is a fourth group of mothers that we do not get to see. These are the mothers who range from being bored by their children to those who really dislike their children.

As a consequence this group ranges from those who ignore their children (beyond feeding and clothing them) to those that are child abusers even to the point of killing them. The fact that we do not get to see or know this last group of mothers is hardly surprising.

On a television talk show not long ago a fellow guest, who was a newsman, said to me, "Feeling as you do about children, do you believe that couples should be required to have a license before they may have babies?"

I told him that I hadn't ever thought about that but that I would think it over.

I've thought it over since then.

If I thought that governments or agencies were sane enough to exercise the wisdom of Solomon and thus to be 100 percent correct in determining, a priori, who the potential neglecters, abusers or murderers were, it wouldn't be a bad idea. I do not have sufficient faith in governments to believe such wisdom exists.

Besides, I have a strong suspicion that a good many women who are bored with or who dislike children before becoming mothers turn out to be first-rate mothers and first-rate human beings *after* the baby is born.

The arrival of a newborn baby does marvelous things to us grown-ups.

Happily that fourth group of parents, the ones we don't get to see, is very small.

The first group of mothers, the ones who wish to spend full time with their children and who are fortunate enough to be able to do so, can and do multiply their babies' intelligences when they know of how to do so.

The second group of mothers can and do multiply their babies' intelligences when they have the knowledge to do so. Perhaps on average they are able to spend three or four hours a day with their babies. That gives them enough time to teach their babies how to read, to gain encyclopedic knowledge and to do math. This permits them to multiply and not simply add to their own babies' intelligence and thus to grow the brains of their babies.

This group of mothers are less likely to have the time to teach their babies how to play the violin, speak several languages (unless the parents happen to be bilingual) or to teach their babies gymnastics.

I am often bemused by all the talk today that because a large number of mothers in today's society must go out to work they can't spend all day teaching their children.

The implication of that statement is that because my own old-fashioned mother did not go out to work, she had nothing to do other than teach her children all day long.

The idea that during the quarter of a century which my mother devoted to raising her children she had nothing else to do would amuse Mother (and all of her contemporaries) a great deal. During most of those twenty-five years, Mother had no electric washing machine, gas or electric stove, electric sewing machine or automatic furnace, never mind a toaster, dishwasher, garbage disposal, mixer, can opener, or air conditioner.

So in addition to raising three kids my mother had a few other things to do at the same time, such as sewing by hand, darning socks, stoking a coal furnace, preparing meals on a coal stove, washing clothes by hand and so on and so on and so on, until late at night. It is true that mother did not go out to work during the years she raised us.

It is not true that she didn't work.

So it was with every other mother and kid I knew until I was eighteen.

Nor do I wish to imply that we were either poor or uneducated people. Mother had managed to attend the state teacher's college, which was then known as a "normal school.". Dad earned what passed as a good salary in those years of the Great Depression and spent every spare cent on books, which he loved and which filled our tiny house.

My guess is that my mother and the other mothers of that day had a good deal less than four hours a day to devote to each of their children.

Mothers have always had a good deal more to do than only teaching their babies. The miracle is that they have managed to do such an extraordinary job in the small amounts of time they have had to do it.

What then of that third group of mothers who have very small amounts of time to spend with their babies? Is it possible for them to multiply their babies' intelligences as this book proposes?

Those mothers, when they wish to do so, need this book and what it teaches the most of all.

It has become almost trite to say that what matters most is not so much the amount of time we may spend with our babies but rather the quality of time we spend with them.

Of course the quality of the time we spend

with our children is important. But the quantity of time is also important.

We live in a society that wants to believe that it is possible for its women to be all things to all people.

This is not possible.

The idea that it is possible to be a kind of super mom who has a full time profession outside the home and who is able to provide her children with the same mothering that she received from her own full time mother when she was a child is, of course, nonsense.

It can't be done.

Indeed, it is very unfair to expect any woman to do it. No one wants to say this because it means that we as individuals and as a society must decide between the future of our children and what we may see as our own professional future.

In a saner society, when a woman decides that she is going to have a baby she should be able to take six years (not six months) to be with her child. She could then return to being whatever it is that she was doing before she had her baby.

Many, many professional women have done just that. They say that the experience of being a full time mother was the most important job they ever had. Further they say that they are much better doctors or lawyers or whatever now than they were before they stopped to become professional mothers.

Six years is a very short period of time in an adult's life but for a child these six years will never come again.

How tragic for our society that too often mother and father work long hours to provide their children with a good material existence. But as a result the tiny child sees very little of his parents when he needs them the most.

Then when we have established the material security which has preoccupied us, we want to spend time with our children, who are by now young adults. Now it is they who do not have time for us. We realize too late that we have missed the boat. Maybe that second car or those vacations were not as important as we thought.

There is definitely some important rethinking that needs to be done by each of us and by our society about the lives of our babies between birth and six years of life.

Everyone should know, in their heart of hearts, that taking tiny children away from their mothers and putting them with dozens of other tiny kids who have also been separated from their mothers is a bad idea.

Everyone should know it but no one wants to say it.

Our present work force has been built on the assumption that tiny children don't need to be with their mothers and can be herded together like little sheep and everything will work out just fine.

This is a lie.

Quality time is good but there is no substitute for one mother and father for each child.

There never has been and there never will be.

The younger a child is the more important it is that both quantity of time and quality of time be high.

Mothers are the best teachers and so are fathers.

If everything goes well in the world, they will continue to be.

Charles Simmons once said, "If you would reform the world from its errors and vices, begin by enlisting the mothers."

We began enlisting the help of mothers over three decades ago and we have never regretted it.

The world, as anybody who reads a newspaper anywhere in the world knows, could use a good deal of reform from its errors and vices.

It would not be difficult to make a case for the belief that the world is as nutty as a Christmas fruit cake.

There are those who question whether it makes any sense to raise highly competent and eminently sane children who will grow up to live in a world which is essentially insane.

If one thinks about that a bit it becomes clearer that raising highly competent and completely sane children is the *only* possible hope for making an insane world sane.

The world itself, in its normal state of nature, is not only totally sane but beautifully ordered.

It is humans alone who make the world sane or insane. What other way could there possibly be to create a sane world for tomorrow morning than to raise totally sane children?

For the children of the world are what tomorrow morning is made of, and tomorrow morning will arrive—tomorrow morning.

We human beings are the stuff of which dreams are made.

14

geniuses—
not too many
but too few

When a true genius appears in the world
you may know him by this sign,
that the dunces are all in confederacy
against him.

—JONATHAN SWIFT

As with mothers, the myths about geniuses are legion and they would be hysterically funny if they weren't so libelous.

I suspect that none of the myths about geniuses were invented by geniuses; they were invented by people who were less than geniuses—and that ought to give us our first clue as to why they were invented.

Certainly one of the most common myths about geniuses is "Geniuses, because they are geniuses, have great problems."

We would like to begin the discussion of that one by asking you to set this myth aside long enough to draw on your own experience to answer this question: "Who have problems, geniuses or chowder-heads?"

Since we all have friends in both groups, let's check this against our own experience.

At the Institutes we are lucky enough to be rich in genius friends and I find it thrilling and a great happiness to be able to be with them. Every cell in me snaps to attention and my mind boggles as I listen to them. I even enjoy venturing ideas and opinions and find myself feeling perfectly comfortable when I do so, since I find geniuses to be both good and attentive listeners. They are tremendously curious about everything.

I also have many chowder-headed friends. They are primarily people with whom I grew up in the several neighborhoods in which I have lived and in the wartime army. Among the people with whom I grew up, I found some chowder-heads and, less often, I found a genius in those places.

I enjoy being with my chowder-headed friends also, but for very different reasons. My enjoyment with them is mainly due to how very relaxing I find it to be. I lean back, put up my feet, and I ask, "Do you think it will rain?"

After due thought, somebody ventures an opinion.

"Yes, I think it will."

There is an audible groan in the group.

After another period of sober thought, another friend ventures an opinion.

"No, I don't think it will."

Everyone brightens considerably.

And that's that.

There are only two possibilities. It either will, or it won't. We have just covered all possibilities, and we may now relax and consider gravely the profundity of the question.

One might be led to conclude that these are farmer friends of mine. Not so. They are city friends and I find they are almost uniformly opposed to it raining—ever!

So, for very different reasons, I enjoy being with my genius friends and with my chowder-headed friends.

I also find myself less willing to express either my ideas or my opinions among my chowder-headed friends. I find them to be far less tolerant of either opinions or ideas than are my genius friends.

They also have far more problems than do my genius friends.

It is chowder-heads and not geniuses who have problems.

We shall return to them and to their greatest frustration, the rain, shortly.

Another common concern about geniuses is that they are extremely frustrated people and, as everyone knows, it is very bad to be frustrated.

During the last several decades we have all been treated to a good deal more psychobabble than most of us wish to be subjected to in a very long lifetime.

Not the least of the disservices that this drivel has forced upon us is the near destruction of the meaning of some perfectly fine words and a search for a world which, if we ever succeed in finding it, will prove to be a total disaster.

High among the good words which have been twisted into evil are the words "stress," "frustration" and "aggression."

We are in constant search for a pill which will eliminate all stress in us, and rich will be the drug company which first produces such a pill—but not, I think, for long.

Can you imagine having taken such a pill just before trying to cross Times Square on a Saturday night, walking on a high plateau in a severe lightning storm during a driving rain, or trying to get out of a burning house?

How about those evil words, frustration and aggression?

Geniuses, by and large, are the most frustrated, aggressive and fulfilled people in the world.

What is wrong is the assumption that a sense of frustration and the act of aggression are necessarily bad. They are not.

Everyone alive is frustrated and aggressive to the degree that he is struck by the difference between the way things *are* in this world and the way things *ought* to be.

The less bright and caring one is, the less one is struck by this difference.

The more bright and caring one is, the more one is struck by the difference between how things are and how they ought to be.

Given that virtually everyone is frustrated by this difference, we can then measure the size of us by two things.

We can measure how much we care about humanity by the nature and the size of the problems which frustrate us.

We can measure our abilities and our worth by what we do about them.

I can measure the size of my chowder-headed friends by what frustrates them. They are frustrated by the fact that it rains.

Frustration, as everyone knows, leads to aggression.

We can measure our abilities and our worth by what we do about it.

We can measure the size of the geniuses by the size of the problems which frustrate them.

If I were asked to list the ten greatest physicians in history, starting with Christ or Mohammed, I should have to include Jonas Salk in the list.

Jonas Salk has virtually eliminated that hateful disease Infantile Paralysis. He obviously couldn't stand the idea that little children who hadn't harmed anyone should be killed or maimed by polio. That created great frustration in him.

In 1940, at the height of that disease, I was a physical therapist.

In those days, physical therapists were primarily concerned with flying around the country to the latest outbreak of polio and trying to treat it. I also hated and was frustrated by that dreadful disease. My frustrations led to my being very aggressive. I tried to solve the problem by treating it, but treatment had little or no effect.

Jonas Salk's frustration led to aggression and his aggression led to trying to prevent polio. By his genius, he succeeded. Polio is now so rare that little children, and many young adults, have never even heard of it.

Isn't that wonderful?

The result of his frustration, which led to his aggression, was success. Jonas Salk must be one of the most fulfilled of human beings. Can one imagine greater fulfillment than having purged the earth of one of the greatest scourges which has beset children?

Now may I return to the frustrations and the aggressions of my friends the chowder-heads? They are frustrated by rain (and other such imagined calamities). This leads them to be aggressive about it. Where then do their aggressions lead them? What do they do?

They complain.

By the size of the problems which frustrate us and by what we do about them shall we be known.

It is true that geniuses—like everyone else—are frustrated.

And we can thank the Good Lord, and them, for that.

How about another myth about geniuses? It says that geniuses are very often very ineffective and highly impractical people.

We have the well-known example of the great genius who, despite his genius, is an ineffectual bumbler who never accomplishes anything in life.

Yes, he is well known but non-existent. Well known but never seen. This non-existent bumbling genius cannot exist because he is an obvious contradiction in terms. It is not possible simultaneously to be a genius and to be ineffectual.

We have often seen these people who are reputed to be brilliant chowder-heads. They are easy to explain. They are not ineffectual geniuses. They are ineffectual people who have been misdiagnosed as geniuses. They are mistakes in testing.

They are living, breathing, walking, talking proof that the traditional, presently-used tests of intelligence do not measure intelligence.

We can't be intelligent (having a good mental capacity, quick to understand, showing distinctive comprehension, sagacious, understanding, sensible, knowing, astute, shrewd, brainy, clever, discerning, alert, acute, quick, bright, apt, keen sighted, sharp sighted, clear eyed, sharp witted, clear headed, rational, smart, penetrating, perceptive, ingenious, etc.) and be bumbling at the same time. Now can we?

This fellow is not apocryphal. He's real. He just isn't a genius. He is often highly educated and knowledgeable, skilled at taking tests which test his knowledge but not his intelligence. He's proof that the old I.Q. tests don't work.

Genius is as genius does.

Leonardo is known as a genius for all the superb things he did. He obviously never took an I.Q. test.

So also are all the great geniuses of history known for what they did, not for how they scored on an I.Q. test. Very few of them ever took an I.Q. test.

Suppose that they had. If they had had an average I.Q. score, would we stop reading Shakespeare's plays or listening to Beethoven's music? Would things fall up if Newton's I.Q. had been less than genius? Would the lights go out if Edison had been stupid, as he was reported to have been as a child?

Edison is a good example. Edison was a precocious reader, having been taught to read by his mother. He did poorly in school. So do most geniuses. He didn't do poorly because he was stupid. He did poorly because he was bright and therefore bored. His headmaster warned that he would never make a success of anything.

Edison was not stupid. Edison was a genius. He patented over a thousand inventions.

It was not Edison who was wrong. It was Edison's teachers who were wrong.

Albert Einstein performed so badly in high school that his teachers advised him to drop out: "You'll never amount to anything."

Almost all geniuses hated school. They were bored.

Some mothers ask, "If I teach my child to

read before he goes to school, won't he be bored when he goes to school?"

This question is easy to answer. Unless he goes to an extraordinarily fine and very unusual school, you can bet your boots he'll be bored in school. If he's very bright, he will be bored in school. If he's average, he will be bored in school. If he's not very bright, he'll be bored in school.

All children are bored in school.

That's because schools are boring. They are insulting to children's intelligence.

The question is not, "Will they be bored?" They will be bored.

The question is, "How can one deal with boredom?"

At first glance it seems strange to appreciate that the brighter people are, the more they dislike boredom—but the better they deal with it.

Children deal brilliantly with boredom, and the brighter they are, the better they deal with it.

Does it take a great deal of thought to determine whether a genius or a dope would survive better if alone on a desert island?

Consider the alternatives.

Would it really have been better if Einstein, Edison and all the others like them had been dull, and therefore less bored in school? Would it have been better for them? Better for the world?

Would you rather have your own child dull enough not to be bored in school?

I personally spent four hundred and eleven years in first grade. Didn't you? Don't you remember how long it was between 8:30 a.m. and recess at 11:30 a.m.?

A very bright Australian mother who had taught her children to read was introducing me to her one-month old baby. I poked my finger into the baby's belly and said, "Hey, baby, how are you?"

With a very bright twinkle in her eye, Mother said, "Oh, don't talk to the baby. If he learns to talk too soon, he might be bored in school." I chuckled all the way to Sydney.

It's the school system which needs changing, not the kids.

Making your child highly capable and highly intelligent will help make him "school proof." All the geniuses were.

One thing is clear. If three children out of thirty children in the first grade go to school already reading, doing math and having encyclopedic knowledge, there will be at least three children who will enter the second grade reading, doing math and with encyclopedic knowledge.

It isn't the children who can read who have problems, it's the children who can't who have problems.

It isn't geniuses who have problems, it's the chowder-heads who have problems.

Chauncey Gay Suits pointed out that "Children share with geniuses an open, enquiring, uninhibited quality of mind."

The myth which says that there is a thin line between genius and insanity—is a myth.

It is reasonable to suppose that being a genius does not insure against psychosis. The question is, "Does being a genius somehow lead to psychosis?"

All of our observations of the full spectrum of human function lead us to exactly the opposite view. We have been privileged to know many of the geniuses of our time and we have found them to be the sanest people we know.

Does anyone believe that high intelligence would lead to killing the President of the United States, shooting the Pope or killing six million people in concentration camps?

We have already dealt with the insanity of the term "evil genius". It is a contradiction in terms.

If your child is very bright, will he be happy? That depends a lot on what you mean by happiness.

If it is proper to define happiness as the absence of unhappiness, then we know a great many happy people, but they are all in institutions staring at blank walls, and they are known as idiots.

Perhaps the absence of unhappiness is not a good definition of happiness.

True geniuses are the happiest, kindest, sanest, most caring, most effective people around. That's how we know they are geniuses.

Could any sane human being be happy while reading the front page of a newspaper?

Perhaps a better definition of happiness would be the state which follows when, after reading the newspaper, one does something which helps to reverse what one just read on the front page of a newspaper.

Now finally, let's consider that group of geniuses who are known as "little kids." This is the last, but certainly not the least, of the myths about geniuses.

Little geniuses are nasty and hateful.

For more than thirty years we have been faced with children who have performed at superior levels. We have lived with them and with their parents. Some of them have been well children and some of them have been brain-injured, but what is true of all of them is this: almost without exception, the brighter they are, the more thoughtful and lovable they have been.

The brighter the kids, the fewer they have of those characteristics which occasionally make us wish to throttle kids. The brighter they are, the less likely they are to whine, cry, complain, hit and be otherwise obnoxious. They have no such need.

The brighter they are, the richer they are in all the characteristics for which we love children.

They are, in addition, more curious, more independent, more capable of taking care of themselves. They are more confident, more self-assured, more conscious of their own worth and have highly developed personalities. They are their own people. They are very interesting people who respect others and expect to be respected in turn.

That's the way it is. It isn't up for grabs, it is simply the way it is. They're the facts as we see them daily—year in and year out.

It is good—not bad—to be a genius.

The world does not have too many geniuses —it has too few.

15

how to use 30 seconds

Having hated math in school, I did not even know about the law of combinations and permutations until I grew up. Then I learned about it by accident and found it very exciting.

In the event you missed this too, let's devote a page or two to it because understanding this law is vital to appreciating the astonishing things you can do with your baby in thirty seconds.

If I have five pencils, each of a different color,

I am able to set them up in a surprising number of different combinations. I can put the red one with the blue one, the red one with the yellow one, the red one with the green one, the green one with the yellow pencil, the green pencil with the blue one and so on.

Mathematicians have a formula for this. It is 5 x 4 x 3 x 2 x 1 which amount to 120 ways to combine the five pencils.

Now if I make it six pencils, the number becomes more than surprising since there are 720 ways to combine six objects.

The number of ways I can combine seven (and now I'm forced to my annoyingly capable little calculator) is astonishing—5,040.

Nine is mind-boggling—362,880.

Ten is—3,628,800.

Eleven is—39,916,800

And 12 stumps even my little calculator, which doesn't go that high.

The basis of all intelligence is facts.

Without facts there can be no intelligence.

Let's check that out in two ways, with computers and with human beings.

A three million dollar computer which has just arrived from the manufacturer is empty of facts. It can answer nothing. It is said to be in a zero state. If we want it to answer questions, we must do three things.

1. We must present it with facts. We can put one fact in each of its memory cells. These facts are called "bits of information." They must meet three requirements. They must be:
   a. Precise
   b. Discrete
   c. Non-ambiguous
2. We must program the computer in such a way that it can manipulate these facts with each other in order to derive new answers.
3. We must teach it a language in which to answer our questions.

The computer will now be limited to answering questions which can be derived from the facts which we have taught it.

If we put in a small number of facts we can get back only a small number of answers.

If we put in a large number of facts we can get back a larger number of answers.

If we put in a huge number of facts we can get back a huge number of answers.

The number of facts we can store is limited to the number of memory cells it contains.

If we store in a single memory cell the number "one" we now have nothing more than a bank. We may ask the computer to tell us what we told it.

If we store another number "one" in another

memory cell we may now ask the computer several questions. What is one plus one? What is two minus one?

If we store another "one" in another cell the number of questions we may ask rises sharply. What is one plus one? What is one plus two? What is one plus one plus one? What is three minus two? What is three minus one? And so on.

As we add each new fact the number of answers we may derive rises, not on an arithmetic curve but at an exponential rate.

If we put in garbled information we will get garbled answers.

The computer people have a superb saying.

"G.I.G.O."

That means "Garbage in—Garbage out."

Because this is obvious we would not dream of allowing an unskilled human being to program a computer. We therefore spend a great deal of time and money sending human beings to school to learn how to program computers.

We deal with computers with a respect which approaches awe.

The greatest computers which exist have an intelligence estimated by the computer people to be about that of an insect called the earwig. (The earwig is not famous for its intelligence).

Now let's consider that incredible computer,

the child's brain, which weighs three pounds and has a capacity ten times greater than that of the National Archives of the United States.

The computer works on the same basis as the human brain and was, of course, modeled on the human brain. Up to now computers are startling but remain very poor copies of the human brain.

The human brain which has no facts is said to be an idiot.

Let's take a clear example. If we take an earthworm (which has a tiny brain indeed) and slowly cut off a piece of it on a laboratory table, it will do everything in its very limited power to prevent our doing so.

What happens to a human child who is in a profound coma under the same circumstance?

Coma, by definition, is a state of unconsciousness in which the human being is functionally deaf, functionally blind and functionally insensate.

If one took a dull saw and slowly cut a leg off a human being who was in a profound coma, he would not object in any way.

Surely there can be no clearer example of a total lack of intelligence than one in which a human being does not object to being dismembered.

Why?

Is it that he is unable to move or make sounds?

It is a great deal more basic than that. The fact is not that he can't object, but rather that he does not know you are cutting off his leg.

He can't see you cutting it off.

He can't hear you cutting it off.

He can't feel you cutting it off.

He can't smell you cutting it off.

He can't taste you cutting it off.

He has no facts at his disposal. Without facts there can be no intelligence.

It is important to note that if we arouse the child so that he no longer is in coma, and assuming that he was well prior to being in coma, he may then demonstrate an I.Q. of 137. This makes clear the difference between functional intelligence and potential intelligence.

The Institutes have many reasons to know about coma since for years its staff have been arousing comatose children who would otherwise die or vegetate.

You will not be surprised to learn that the staff does so by giving the child in coma visual, auditory and tactile stimulation with greatly increased frequency, intensity and duration, in recognition of the orderly way in which the brain grows.

Indeed the late Dr. Edward LeWinn of the

Institutes' staff revised the technical definition of coma in his book, *Coma Arousal: The Family As A Team* (Doubleday, 1985). He altered the definition slightly, but its meaning significantly.

Medical dictionaries define coma as "a state of unconsciousness from which the patient can not be aroused."

Dr. LeWinn defines coma as, "a state of unconsciousness from which the patient has not yet *been* aroused."

Without facts there can be no intelligence.

A single example should make this clear. Let's suppose you are reading this book sitting in your living room. Suppose that at this minute a fire has started in your basement.

As important as we believe this book to be, you should not be reading it if a fire has begun in your house. The only intelligent thing to do would be to put it out or call the Fire Department or both. If you continue to read you are not taking intelligent action. Question: how do you know that a fire is not starting in your basement?

Clearly we can take no intelligent action without facts.

The human brain is the most superb of all computers and obeys the same rules. With a small number of facts it can come to a small number of conclusions. With an average number of facts it can come to an average number of conclusions. With a huge number of facts it can come to a huge number of conclusions.

If they are *related* facts the number of conclusions is breathtaking.

We have the same requirements as does the computer. If we put garbage into our children's brains we shall get garbage out. In referring to this presentation of facts to children we prefer to refer to an individual fact as a *Bit of Intelligence*, rather than a bit of information. A *Bit of Intelligence* must be:

Precise
Discrete
Non-ambiguous

What things can we do with thirty seconds?
What can we not do with thirty seconds!
Let's consider what different parents can do with thirty seconds.
A child looks out the window and says, "What's that?"

Possibility Number One:
We can say, "Sorry baby. Mommy has to get dinner."
It will take at least thirty seconds to get rid of the baby and make that stick.

Possibility Number Two:

We can look out the window and say, "That's a bow-wow."

It will take at least thirty seconds to make that one stick.

Of all the ridiculous ways we arrogant adults have of wasting a child's precious time and brain, few compare to doing so by teaching him two or three vocabularies of words which range from cloying to obscene. At a later time we will wallop him if he uses the words of his earlier vocabulary.

We use such silly words to describe dogs, cats, birds, urine, bowel movements, sexual organs and a host of other things.

Consider the number of words we teach him at various stages to mean "penis." How about starting right out with calling it a penis? Not a bad word really.

Possibility Number Three:

We can use thirty seconds to say, "That's a dog."

It will take at least thirty seconds to make that one stick. At least it's true to say, "That's a dog."

However, it is far from meeting the standards.

The word "dog" is not precise, it is not discrete and it is highly ambiguous. If one says the word "dog" to a hundred different people, a hundred different images will appear in the mind, ranging from tiny brown smooth ones to huge black and white hairy ones. It will range from the image of a beloved friend to a frightening enemy.

Possibility Number Four:
We can say, "That's a dog called a Saint Bernard."

We can then go on to give him thirty seconds' worth of information which is precise, discrete and non-ambiguous and true.

Number Four is a fine answer and meets the requirements.

How sad it is that we put information into a computer with great skill and great precision and put information into our children's brains in a hit-or-miss, slip-shod, sloppy and often untruthful way.

Remember also, that unlike the computer, we can never totally erase the facts which we put into our baby's brain. They will remain as the first response available on recall. They will remain if they are true and they will remain if they are untrue.

What is the moon made of?

Did I hear you say, "green cheese?" If you didn't, you probably are not of British ancestry. That's a British lie. Other children get Spanish, or French, or Italian, or Japanese, or African or Chinese lies.

Is that the extent of what you can do with thirty seconds? Even if you used the fourth and proper method it is only the beginning.

Words are facts, numbers are facts and pictures are facts, especially if they are precise, discrete, non-ambiguous and, of course, to be facts they must be true.

In the chapters on reading, encyclopedic knowledge and math which follow we will tell you exactly what precise, discrete and non-ambiguous mean as well as how to make the materials for presenting them to children.

For now, suffice it to say, most encyclopedic facts are presented on cardboard which is 11" x 11" in size and on each of these cards is a large clear picture of the thing to be presented. The thing might be a kind of dog, bird, insect, reptile, mineral, President of the United States, work of art and so on through dozens of subjects.

Now let's see what we can do with thirty seconds divided into three ten second periods on three consecutive days.

In ten seconds a skilled mother can show her child, who is familiar with the way it is done, ten different pictures. The faster mother does it, the better the child will learn.

"Bluebird"
"St. Bernard"
"Rattlesnake"
"Emerald"
"President Kennedy"
"Tanzania"
"Beethoven"
"Shakespeare"
"Brazilian Flag"
"French Horn"
Ten seconds—ten facts.

If mother does them on three consecutive days using one second per card the child will be well on his way to having ten superbly clear facts stored in permanent storage.

So—in thirty seconds we can give him ten wonderful facts in contrast to saying, "Get lost" or, "Bow-wow."

Is that the end of it? It is hardly the beginning.

To give you the complete picture and to make it understandable we must make a supposition which is actually improbable but which in no way invalidates the point we should like to make. Suppose your child were a perfectly normal two-year-old who had never seen a dog in his life.

Now you are going to have one of the ten second teaching sessions you both love.

You have prepared ten *Bit of Intelligence* cards each of which contains a clear and first-rate picture of a breed of dog.

These ten cards are different from the previous ten in that they are all dogs. In short, they are ten *related facts*. They are like ten pencils of different colors.

Here you go with your ten seconds and ten pictures of different kinds of dogs.

"Bobby these are all pictures of animals called 'dogs.'"

"Dachshund"

"Collie"

"Labrador Retriever"

"Schnauzer"

"Cocker Spaniel"

"German Shepherd"

"Boxer"

"Doberman Pinscher"

"Samoyed"

"Pekinese"

Ten seconds—three consecutive days, thirty seconds.

Now you go out on the street with Bobby who has never actually seen a dog and down the street comes a Chesapeake Bay Retriever. Does anybody doubt for a moment that Bobby will point excitedly and say, "Mommy, Mommy, a DOG."

Don't doubt it. He will.

He will not of course say, "Chesapeake Bay Retriever."

He has never seen or heard of that kind of dog. But he has heard of and seen dogs. He has learned them superbly. But how it it possible for him to recognize this dog, even as a dog?

You have taught him ten dogs. He knows all the things that dogs have in common. Four legs, heads, tails, hair, etc. He also knows that dogs come in many colors, with big ears, little ears, short tails, long tails, hairy, shaggy, smooth and so on.

You have given him ten dogs which he has now combined and permutated. He has exactly three million, six hundred twenty-eight thousand, eight hundred ways of combining and permutating them.

Are you thunder-struck?

If you're not, then we've presented the case poorly indeed.

Has he got room for all of that?

Remember his capacity is one hundred and twenty-five trillion.

Remember also that his brain grows by precisely this kind of use.

Are you saying, "But surely he'll never use the whole 3,628,800 of the combinations he can make with ten dogs."

Perhaps not. If you'd tell us how many and which ones he is going to use, perhaps we can find a way to teach him just those. But why should we limit him?

Ever buy a dictionary or an encyclopedia? How many words or facts have you ever actually looked up? A thousand? Why didn't you just buy a book that only had the thousand you were going to use? Were you ever out of your house where you kept the dictionary or encyclopedia and wished you had it?

How would you like to have an encyclopedia in your head, especially knowing that the brain grows by use?

Is having a huge number of facts, then, all there is to it? Of course not. We all have met somebody in our lives who has a head full of facts and doesn't have enough sense to come in out of the rain.

But that doesn't alter the fact that the degree of intelligence we have will be limited to the things which can be determined from the number of facts we have.

We have only begun to talk about how.

Let's summarize what you can do with thirty seconds. In answer to his original question, you can:

1.   Tell him to get lost

2.   Tell him it's a bow-wow
3.   Tell him it's a dog
4.   Tell him it's a St. Bernard
5.   Teach him ten superb facts
6.   Teach him ten related facts.

If you choose the sixth possibility you will have given him 3,628,800 ways to combine and permutate those ten facts, and grown his brain in the process.

By the way, he now has eleven facts. He knows there is a family of creatures called dogs, much like his own family is called Smith.

You can also give him the fact that in Latin that family of dogs is called *cane.* That would give him 12 facts to begin with. Let's see, 12 x 11 x 10 x—well it doesn't fit on my little calculator.

THAT'S what you can do with thirty seconds.

Feel good?

16

how to teach
your baby

We mothers are the potters and our children the clay.

—WINIFRED SACKVILLE STONER,
Natural Education

Most sets of instructions begin by saying that
unless they are followed precisely, they won't
work.

In contrast, it is almost safe to say that no
matter how poorly you expose your baby to
reading, encyclopedic knowledge or mathematics he is almost sure to learn more than he
would if you hadn't done it; so this is one game
which you will win to some degree no matter
how badly you play it. You would have to do it

incredibly badly to produce no result.

Nonetheless, the more cleverly you play the game of teaching your tiny child the quicker and the better your child will learn.

Let's review the cardinal points to remember about the child himself before discussing how to teach him.

1. By the age of five a child can easily absorb tremendous amounts of information. If he is younger than five it will be easier. If the child is younger than four it will be even easier and more effective, before three even easier and much more effective and before two is the easiest and most effective of all.

2. The child before five can accept information at a remarkable rate.

3. The more information a child absorbs before the age of five, the more he retains.

4. The child before five has a tremendous amount of energy.

5. The child before five has a monumental desire to learn.

6. The child before five can learn anything that you can teach in an honest and factual and joyous way and *wants* to learn anything that is taught in that way.

7. All tiny children are linguistic geniuses.

8. The child before five learns an entire language and can learn as many languages as are presented to him.

This book covers three major areas of intellectual growth and development: reading, encyclopedic knowledge and mathematics.

The first area is reading and of the three it is by far the most important. Reading is one of the highest functions of the human brain—of all creatures on earth, only humans can read.

Reading is one of the most important functions in life, since virtually all formal learning is based on the ability to read.

You should begin with reading. Once you have been doing a good consistent reading program for a while then you should begin your encyclopedic knowledge program.

All human intelligence is based upon facts which constitute human knowledge. Without facts *there can be no intelligence.*

You should begin your encyclopedic knowledge program by evolution using several categories of *Bit of Intelligence* cards. When this is going well and you are feeling restless to begin a new area then you begin your mathematics program.

As you will see, mathematics is really a natural subdivision of any good comprehensive program since you begin with mathematical *Bit of Intelligence* cards—the dot cards.

The purpose of this chapter is to outline the basic principles of good teaching. These principles apply to reading, encyclopedic knowledge and mathematics, as well as to anything else you may wish to teach your child.

We are so much a product of our own educations that sometimes in teaching our children we unwittingly make the same mistakes that were the cause of so much suffering for us.

Schools often arrange for children to fail. We can all remember the big red X's on all the wrong answers. Correct answers often received no mention at all. Tests were often given with the intention of exposing our ignorance rather than discovering our knowledge.

In order to enjoy the unalloyed thrill of teaching your tiny child, it is best to begin with a clean slate.

Here are the guidelines—the basics of good

teaching—to help you to succeed.

At What Age to Begin

You can really begin the process of teaching your baby right from birth. After all, we speak to the baby at birth—this grows the auditory pathway. We can also provide the same information to the visual pathway by teaching him to read using reading cards, teaching him encyclopedic knowledge using *Bit of Intelligence* cards or teaching him to recognize quantities in mathematics using dot cards. All of these things grow the visual pathway substantially.

There are two *vital* points involved in teaching your child.

1. Your attitude and approach.
2. The size and orderliness of the teaching materials.

Parent Attitude and Approach

If teaching your child appeals to you, then go ahead and plunge in. Take your phone off the hook and put a sign on your front door that reads "Silence—Professional Mother At Work—Do Not Disturb."

If you want to become a professional mother, you will be joining the oldest and most venerable profession in the world. If you believe it is a privilege to teach your child, you should avail yourself of that privilege.

If you do not like the idea of teaching your child, indeed, if there is anything about it that feels like a duty, please don't do it.

It will not work. You won't like it. Your child won't like it.

This isn't for everyone.

Learning is the greatest adventure of life. Learning is desirable, vital, unavoidable and, above all, life's greatest and most stimulating game. The child believes this and will always believe this—unless we persuade him that it isn't true.

The primary rule is that both parent and child must joyously approach learning as the superb game that it is.

Those educators and psychologists who say that we must not teach tiny children lest we steal their precious childhood by inflicting learning upon them tell us nothing about a child's attitude toward learning—but they certainly tell us a great deal about what they themselves feel about learning.

The parent must never forget that learning is life's most exciting game—it is *not* work.

Learning is a reward; it is not a punishment.

Learning is a pleasure; it is not a chore.

Learning is a privilege; it is not denial.

The parent must always remember this and must never do anything to destroy this natural attitude in the child.

There is a fail-safe law you must never forget. It is this: If you aren't having a wonderful time and your child isn't having a wonderful time—stop! You are doing something wrong.

Relax and enjoy yourself. This is the greatest game there is. The fact that it results in important changes in your child should not make it "serious" for you. You and your child have nothing to lose and everything to gain.

As your child's teacher, you should make sure that you eat and sleep enough to be relaxed and enjoy yourself. Being tense is usually a result of fatigue, disorganization, or of not having a complete understanding of why you are doing what you are doing,

All of these things are easily remedied and should be if you are not enjoying yourself.

For your child's sake you may have to become a bit more conscientious about your own well-being than you might have been before.

Respect and Trust

Your child trusts you, often completely and absolutely.

Return that trust.

Your child will sense your respect and trust in your attitude, manner and actions.

He wants to learn more than he wants anything in the world.

Give your child the opportunity to learn as a privilege that he has earned.

The things that you are teaching your child are precious.

Knowledge is not valuable; it is *invaluable.*

Once a mother asked us, "Should I give my child a kiss after I have taught him something?"

Of course a mother should kiss her child as often as she likes—the more the better. But the question was a little like asking, "Should I give him a kiss after I kiss him?"

Teaching your child is another kind of kiss.

Now you have another way of showing the most profound form of affection—respect.

Each time you teach your child, the spirit with which you do so should be that of a kiss or a hug.

Your teaching is very much a part of everything you do with your child. It begins when he wakes up and doesn't end until he is sound asleep.

When you have begun your program you should garnish your hard work with the absolute trust that your child has absorbed what you have given him.

Of course he knows what you have told him and shown him. You have gone to some considerable effort to make everything that you teach him nice and clear, and precise, and discrete and non-ambiguous.

What else could he do but know it? It is all so simple for him.

When in Doubt—Bet on Your Child.

If you do you will always be a winner and, what is even more important, so will he.

The whole world is betting against the little child—betting that he doesn't understand, betting that he doesn't remember, betting that he doesn't "get it." Your child doesn't need one more person on that team!

Always Tell Your Child the Truth.

Your child was born thinking that everything that you say is the truth. Never give him any reason to revise his thinking on that subject.

Don't allow anyone else to give him anything less than the truth either. The reason for this should be obvious.

Since you have infinite respect for your child, it is only right that your child should return that respect. If you keep your word in all things and at all times he will respect you. If you do not he may love you but he will not respect you. What a shame it would be to deprive him of that joy.

When Your Child Asks a Question Answer Honestly, Factually and with Enthusiasm.

Your child will quickly come to the conclusion that you have all the answers. He will see you as a source of information. He is right. You are the source of information for him.

When he trusts you with one of his brilliant and usually quite difficult-to-answer questions, rise to the occasion. If you know the answer, give it to him on the spot. Don't put him off if you can possibly avoid it.

If you don't know the answer, tell him you don't know it. Then take the time to find the answer.

Do Not Hesitate to Express Your Own Views.

You are his mother, and although he expects you to give him the facts, he will also need and want your opinions as well.

He will quickly understand when you are giving him hard facts and when you are expressing your own viewpoint, as long as you differentiate between the two.

It is worth remembering that you are not simply teaching your child all that is worth knowing in this world, you are also teaching your grandchildren's father or mother how to teach them.

It is a humbling thought.

The Best Time to Teach

Mother must never play this game unless she *and* her child are happy and in good form. If a child is irritable, tired or hungry it is not a good time to do the program.

For tiny babies teething is often a time of pain and sleeplessness. Never teach your child during such periods. It is a real mistake to think you can teach anything to a human being who is sick, poorly rested, or in pain. If your child is out of sorts find out what is bothering him and handle it.

If mother is cranky or out of sorts, this is not a good time to do the program.

Every mother and child experience days when they are at odds or things just don't seem to be going smoothly.

On a bad day it is best not to play the learning game at all. It is a wise mother who puts away her program on such days, recognizing full well that there are many more happy days than cranky ones and that the joy of learning will be enhanced by choosing the very best and happiest moments to pursue it.

The Best Environment

Provide an environment that is free from visual, auditory and tactile distractions. Most households are not quiet places. However, it is possible to decrease the level of chaos in your house and for the baby's sake it is wise to do so.

Turn off the television, the radio, and the record player while you are teaching. Make an area that is free from the visual chaos of toys, clothing and household clutter. This spot will become your major teaching area.

The Best Duration

Make sure that the length of time you play the game is very short. At first it will be played only a few times a day and each session will involve only a few seconds.

To determine when to end each session of learning, the parent should exercise great foresight.

Always stop before your child wants to stop.

The parent must know what the child is thinking a little bit before the child knows it and must stop.

Always show less material than your child would like to see. Your child should always consider that you are a little bit stingy with his program. There is never enough; consequently, he always wants more.

All tiny children would, if permitted, glut themselves. This is why you get cries of "More!" and "Again!" This is a sure sign of success. You will maintain your success by not giving in to these demands (at least not immediately).

The tyranny of a tiny child can enter in here. When it does, remember you are the mother and as such the teacher of *Bit of Intelligence* cards and reading words, etc. Do not allow your child to set up the dynamics of your program—this is your responsibility. He will not decide wisely—you will.

He is the best learner in the world but *you* are his best teacher.

Promise to come back in five minutes. Ask him to complete something that needs doing first; then you can play the learning game again.

If you always stop before your child wants to stop, he will beg you to play the learning game and you will be nurturing rather than destroying his natural desire to learn.

The Manner of Teaching

Whether a session consists of reading single words, *Bit of Intelligence* cards or math cards, enthusiasm is the key. Do not be subtle with your tiny child.

Use a nice, clear, loud voice infused with all the enthusiasm that you actually feel. It should be easy for your child to hear you and to feel your enthusiasm.

If you have a quiet, unenthusiastic voice—change it.

Create enthusiasm in your voice and your child will absorb it like a sponge. Children love to learn and they do it *very quickly*. Therefore you must show your material *very quickly*.

We adults do almost everything too slowly for

children. There is no area where this is more painfully demonstrated than the way adults teach little children.

Generally we expect a child to sit and stare at his materials and to look as if he is concentrating on them. We actually expect him to look a bit unhappy in order to demonstrate that he is really learning.

But children don't think learning is painful, grown-ups do.

When you show your cards, do so as fast as you can. You will become more and more expert at this as you do it. Practice a bit on father until you feel comfortable.

It is absolutely vital to your success that you zoom through your materials. Speed and enjoyment are inextricably linked in the learning process.

Anything that speeds the process will raise enjoyment. Anything that slows it down will decrease enjoyment.

A slow session is a deadly session. It is an insult to the learning ability of a tiny child and will be interpreted as such by him.

The materials are carefully designed to be large and clear so that you can show them very quickly and your child will see them easily.

Sometimes when a mother speeds up she is apt to become a bit mechanical and lose the natural enthusiasm and "music" in her voice.

It *is* possible to maintain enthusiasm *and* good meaningful sound *and* go very quickly all simultaneously.

It is important that you do so.

Your child's interest and enthusiasm for learning will be closely related to three things.

1. The speed at which materials are shown;
2. The amount of new material;
3. The joyous manner of mother.

The more speed, the more new material and the more joy—the better.

This point of speed, all by itself, can make the difference between a successful session and one that is too slow for your very eager, bright child.

Children don't stare—they don't *need* to stare—they absorb and they do so instantly, like sponges.

Introducing New Material

It is wise at this point to talk about the rate at which each child should learn to read, or absorb encyclopedic knowledge, or recognize pure quantity in mathematics or, for that matter, learn anything.

Don't be afraid to follow your child's lead. You may be astonished at the size of his hunger and at the rate at which he learns.

New information is the spice of every program. It is the most easily overlooked ingredient of success.

When new information is plentiful, you and your child will be flying along. There will never be enough hours in a day or days in a week.

Your child's world will be in a constant state of expansion. This is what every child is aiming for, every day of his life.

We adults were raised in a world that taught us that one must memorize twenty facts perfectly. We drilled these facts over and over. We must learn and be tested at 100 percent or else.

For most of us this endless drilling on a very narrow body of information was the beginning of the end of our attention and interest in whatever the subject may have been.

Instead of 100 percent of twenty how about 50 percent of two thousand?

You don't need to be a mathematical genius to know that one thousand facts are a great deal more than twenty.

But the real point here is not merely that children can learn fifty times more than we offer them.

The important point is what happens when

you show the twenty-first fact or the two thousand and first fact. This is where the secret of teaching very young children lies.

In the former case the effect of the introduction of the twenty-first fact (when a child has seen the first twenty *ad infinitum* and *ad nauseum*) will be to send him running in the opposite direction as fast as possible.

This is the basic principle that is followed in formal education. We adults are experts on how deadly this approach can be. We lived through twelve years of it.

In the latter case the two thousand and first fact is eagerly awaited. The joy of discovery and learning something new is honored and the natural curiosity and love of learning which is born in every child is fed as it should be.

Unfortunately, one method closes the door on learning, sometimes forever.

Fortunately, the other opens the door wide and secures it against future attempts to close it.

In fact your child will learn a great deal more than 50 percent of what you teach to him.

It is more than likely that he will learn 80 to 100 percent.

But if he only learned 50 percent because you offered him so much he would be intellectually happy and healthy.

And, after all, isn't that the point?

Always be willing to change your approach. Make each day new and exciting. A tiny child changes every single day.

As information comes in at a tremendous rate, he uses that information to put two and two together. This process is taking place all day every day.

Sometimes we get a glimpse of him doing something that he has never done before. At other times we may have an insight into some new way he has of looking at the world.

Whether we are lucky enough to see it or not, his abilities literally *multiply* daily.

Just as you are becoming comfortable with one way of teaching something, he is getting it all figured out and naturally wants something fresh.

You and I like to find a nice cozy rut and stay in it for a while. Tiny kids always want to move ahead.

When you say "Goodnight" to your child each evening you should say "Goodbye." He won't be the same tomorrow.

So when you have a nice routine that you like, you will probably have to toss all the cards up in the air and revamp for the "new kid" who woke up this morning.

Organization and Consistency

It is wise to organize yourself and your materials before you begin because once you begin you will want to establish a consistent program.

Your enjoyment will be largely related to your level of organization. A highly organized mother has a strong sense of purpose about what she is doing. She knows exactly what she has done , how many times she has done it, and when it is time to move on. She has a good supply of new information ready and waiting whenever she needs it.

Very fine would-be professional mothers sometimes fall by the wayside only because they never take the time to sit down and get themselves organized.

What a tragedy this is, because if they did organize themselves, they would discover that they are fine teachers who are being held back by minor organizational problems.

A modest program done consistently and happily will be infinitely more successful than an over-ambitious program that overwhelms mother and therefore occurs very sporadically.

An on-again-off-again program will not be effective. Seeing the materials repeatedly but quickly is vital to mastering them. Your child's enjoyment is derived from real knowledge and this can best be accomplished with a program done daily.

However, sometimes it *is* necessary to put the program away for a few days. This is no problem as long as it does not occur too often. Occasionally it may be vital to put it away for several weeks or even months. For example, a new baby's arrival, moving, traveling or an illness in the family cause major disruptions to any daily routine. During such upheavals it is best to put your program away *completely*. Use this time to read to your child from the classics or visit the zoo or go to museums to see works of art you may already have taught at home.

Do not try to do a halfway program during these times. It will be frustrating for you and your child. When you are ready to go back to a consistent program start back exactly where you left off. Do not go back and start over again.

Whether you decide to do a modest program or an extensive program, do whatever suits you *consistently*. You will see your child's enjoyment and confidence grow daily.

Testing

We have said much about teaching but not much about testing.

Our strongest advice on this subject is do *not* test your child. Babies love to learn but they hate to be tested. In that way they are very like grown-ups.

Testing is the opposite of learning.

It is full of stress.

To teach a child is to give him a delightful gift.

To test him is to demand payment in advance. The more you test him, the slower he will learn and the less he will want to.

The less you test him, the quicker he will learn and the more he will want to learn. Knowledge is the most precious gift you can give your child. Give it as generously as you give him food.

What is a test?

In essence it is an attempt to find out what the child *doesn't* know. It is putting him on the spot by saying, "Can you tell the answer to your father?"

It is essentially disrespectful of the child because he gets the notion that we do not believe he can learn unless he proves that he can over and over again.

The intention of the test is a negative one—it is to expose what the child does not know.

The result of testing is to decrease learning and the *willingness* to learn. Do not test your child and do not allow anyone else to do so either.

Well what is a mother to do? She does not want to test her child, she wants to teach him and give him every opportunity to experience the joy of learning and accomplishment.

Therefore, instead of testing her child she provides problem-solving opportunities.

The purpose of a problem-solving opportunity is for the child to be able to demonstrate what he knows if he wishes to do so.

We will discuss different ways of presenting problem-solving opportunities when we discuss how to teach your child to read, to gain encyclopedic knowledge and to learn mathematics in the following chapters.

Material Preparation

The materials used in teaching your child are simple. They are based on many years of work by a large team of child brain developmentalists who studied how the human brain grows and functions. They are designed in recognition that learning is a *brain* function. They recognize the virtues and limitations of the tiny child's visual apparatus and are designed to meet all of his needs from visual crudeness to visual sophistication and from brain function to brain learning.

All materials should be made on fairly stiff white poster board so that they will stand up under the not-always-gentle handling they will receive.

Materials that are of poor quality, unclear, or so small that they are difficult to see will not be learned easily. This will decrease the pleasure of teaching and learning.

Once you begin to teach your child you will find that your child goes through new material very quickly. No matter how often we emphasize this point with parents, they are always astonished at how quickly their children learn.

We discovered a long time ago that it is best to start out ahead. For this reason, make a generous quantity of reading cards, *Bit of Intelligence* cards and math cards before you begin. Then you will have an adequate supply of new materials on hand and ready to use. If you do not do this, you will find yourself constantly behind.

The temptation to keep showing the same old cards over and over again looms large. If mother succumbs to this temptation it spells disaster for her program. The one mistake a child will not tolerate is to be shown the same materials over and over again long after they should have been retired.

Remember, you do not wish to bore the tiny child.

Be smart—start ahead in material preparation and stay ahead. And if for some reason you do get behind in preparing new materials, do not fill in the gap by showing the same old cards again. Stop your program for a day or a week until you have reorganized and made new material, then begin again where you left off.

Material preparation can be a lot of fun and should be. If you are preparing next month's materials, it will be. If you are preparing tomorrow morning's materials it will not be.

Start out ahead, stay ahead, stop and reorganize if you must, but don't show old materials over and over again.

Summary: The Basics of Good Teaching

1. Begin as young as possible.
2. Be joyous at all times.
3. Respect and trust your child.
4. Teach only when you and your child are happy.
5. Create a good learning environment.
6. Stop before your child wants to stop.
7. Introduce new materials often.
8. Be organized and consistent.

9. Do not test your child

10. Prepare your materials carefully and stay ahead.

11. Remember the Fail-Safe Law:

If you aren't having a wonderful time and your child isn't having a wonderful time—stop. You are doing something wrong.

17

how to teach
your baby
to read

Very young children can and do learn to read
words, sentences and paragraphs in exactly the
same way they learn to understand spoken
words, sentences and paragraphs.

Again the facts are simple—beautiful but simple. The eye sees but does not understand what
is seen. The ear hears but does not understand
what is heard.

Only the brain understands.

When the ear hears a spoken word or message,

this message is broken down into a series of electrochemical impulses and flashed to the unhearing brain, which then *comprehends* in terms of the meaning the word was intended to convey.

In the same manner it happens that when the eye sees a printed word or message, this message is broken down into a series of electrochemical impulses and flashed to a brain which understands but does not "see."

It is a magical instrument, the brain.

Both the visual pathway and the auditory pathway travel through the brain where *both* messages are interpreted by the same brain process.

If for any reason a child could be given only a single ability, that single ability should, without any question, be reading.

It is the basis for virtually all formal learning and a large part of informal learning. This chapter will cover the basics of how to teach your baby to read. Parents who wish to have more information about the principles of early reading are advised to read the book *How To Teach Your Baby To Read.*

Material Preparation

The materials used in teaching your child to

read are simple. All materials should be made on fairly stiff white cardboard so that they will stand up under the not-always-gentle handling they will receive.

You will need a good supply of white poster board cut into 4" x 24" strips. If possible purchase these already cut to the size you want. This will save you a lot of cutting, which is much more time consuming than writing words.

You will also need a large red felt-tipped marker. Get the widest tip available. The fatter the marker, the better.

Now write each reading word to be taught on a white poster board strip. Make the letters 3" high. Use lowercase letters except in the case of a proper noun, which of course always begins with a capital letter. Otherwise you will always use lowercase lettering, since this is the way words appear in books.

Make certain your letters are *very* bold. They should be approximately 1/2" wide or wider. This intensity is important to help make it easier for your child to see the word.

Make your lettering neat and clear. Use print, never cursive writing. Make sure you place the word on the card so that there is a border of 1/2" all around the word. This will give you space for your fingers when you hold up the card.

Sometimes mothers get fancy and use stencils to make their cards. This makes beautiful reading cards; however, the time involved is prohibitive.

Your time is precious.

Mothers have to budget time more carefully than members of almost any other profession. You need to develop a fast, efficient means of making your reading cards because you are going to need *a lot* of them.

Neatness and legibility are far more important than perfection. Often mothers find that fathers make very nice cards and appreciate having a hand in the reading program.

Be consistent about how you print. Again your child needs the visual information to be consistent and reliable. This helps him enormously.

The materials begin with large red lower-case letters and progressively change to normal-size black lower-case letters. This is because tiny children have immature visual pathways. The print size of the materials needs to decrease gradually so that the visual pathway may mature through stimulation and use.

The large letters are used initially for the simple reason that they are most easily seen. They are red because red attracts a small child. To start out you may find it simpler to buy a ready-made kit. The How To Teach Your Baby to Read Kit may be obtained by writing to the Better Baby Press.

Once you begin to teach your child to read you will find that your child goes through new material very quickly. As we will repeat this point throughout this book, parents are always astonished at how quickly their children learn.

We discovered a long time ago that it is best to start out ahead. Make at least 200 words before you begin to teach your child. Then you will have an adequate supply of new material on hand and ready to use.

If you do not do this, you will find yourself constantly behind. The temptation to keep showing the same old words over and over again looms large. If mother succumbs to this temptation it spells disaster for her reading program.

The one mistake a child will not tolerate is to be shown the same material over and over again after it should long since have been retired.

Be smart—start ahead in material preparation and stay ahead. And if for some reason you do get behind in preparing new materials, do not fill in the gap by showing the same old words again.

Stop your program for a day or a week until you have reorganized and made new material, then begin again where you left off.

Material preparation can be a lot of fun and should be. If you are preparing tomorrow morning's materials it will not be.

Start out ahead, stay ahead, stop and reorganize if you must, but don't show old materials over and over again.

Let's take a brief look again at the principles of good teaching:

Summary: The Basics of Good Teaching

1. Begin as young as possible.
2. Be joyous at all times.
3. Respect and trust your child.
4. Teach only when you and your child are happy.
5. Create a good learning environment.
6. Stop before your child wants to stop.
7. Introduce new materials often.
8. Be organized and consistent.
9. Do not test your child
10. Prepare your materials carefully and stay ahead.
11. Remember the Fail-Safe Law:

If you aren't having a wonderful time and your child isn't having a wonderful time—stop. You are doing something wrong.

THE READING PATHWAY

The path that you will now follow in order to teach your child is amazingly simple and easy. Whether you are beginning with an infant or a four-year-old the path is essentially the same.

The steps of that path are as follows:

Step One   Single words
Step Two   Couplets
Step Three   Phrases
Step Four   Sentences
Step Five   Books.

STEP ONE *(Single Words)*

The first step in teaching your child to read begins with the use of just fifteen words. When your child has learned these fifteen words he is ready to progress to the vocabularies themselves.

Begin at a time of day when the child is receptive, rested and in a good mood.

Use a part of the house that has as few distracting factors as possible, in both an auditory and visual sense; for instance, do *not* have the radio playing, and avoid other sources of noise. Use a corner of a room which does not have a great deal of furniture, pictures or other objects which might distract the child's vision.

Now simply hold up the word *mommy,* just beyond his reach, and say to him clearly, "This says 'Mommy.'"

Give the child no more description and do not elaborate. Permit him to see it for no more than one second.

Next, hold up the word *daddy* and say, "This says 'Daddy.'"

Show three other words in precisely the same way as you have the first two. Do not ask your child to repeat the words as you go along. After the fifth word, give your child a huge hug and kiss and display your affection in the most obvious ways.

Repeat this three times during the first day, in exactly the manner described above. Sessions should be at least one half-hour apart.

The first day is now over and you have taken the first step in teaching your child to read. (You have thus far invested at most three minutes.)

The second day, repeat the basic session three times. Add a second set of five new words. This new set should be seen three times throughout the day, just like the first set, making a total of six sessions.

At the end of each session tell your child he is very good and very bright. Tell your child that you are very proud of him. Tell him that you love him very much. It is wise to hug him and to express your love for him physically.

Do not bribe him or reward him with cookies, candy or the like. At the rate he will be learning in a very short time, you will not be able to afford enough cookies from a financial standpoint, and he will not be able to take them from a health standpoint. Besides, cookies are a meager reward for such a major accomplishment compared with love and respect.

Children learn at lightning speed and if you show him the words more than three times a day you will bore him. If you show him a single card for more than a second you will lose him.

On the third day, add a third set of five new words.

Now you are teaching your child three sets of reading words, five words in each set, each set three times a day. You and your child are now enjoying a total of nine reading sessions spread out during the day, equaling a few minutes in all.

The first fifteen words that you teach your child should be made up of the most familiar and enjoyable words around him. These words should include the names of immediate family members, relatives, family pets, favorite foods, objects in the house, and favorite activities. It is impossible to include an exact list here since each child's first fifteen words will be personal and therefore different.

The only warning sign in the entire process of learning to read is boredom.

Never bore your child. Going too slowly is much more likely to bore him than going too quickly

Remember that this bright baby can be learning, say, Portuguese at this time, so don't bore him. Consider the splendid thing you have just accomplished. Your child has just conquered the most difficult thing he will have to do in the entire business of reading.

He has done, with your help, two most extraordinary things.

1. He has trained his visual pathway and, more important, his brain, sufficiently to differentiate between one written symbol and another.

2. He has mastered one of the most important abstractions he will ever have to deal with in life: he can read words.

A word about the alphabet. Why have we not

begun by teaching this child the alphabet? The answer to this question is most important.

It is a basic tenet of all teaching that it should begin with the known and the concrete, and progress from this to the new and the unknown, and last of all, to what is abstract.

Nothing could be more abstract to the two-year-old brain than the letter *a*. It is a tribute to the genius of children that they ever learn it.

It is obvious that if the two-year-old were only more capable of reasoned argument he would long since have made this situation clear to adults.

If such were the case, when we presented him with the letter *a*, he would ask, "Why is that thing 'a'?"

What would we answer?

"Well," we would say, "it is 'a' because... uh...because, don't you see it's 'a' because... well, because it was necessary to invent this...ah...symbol to...ah...stand for the sound 'a' which...ah...we also invented so that...ah..."

And so it would have gone.

In the end most of us would surely say, "It's 'a' because I'm bigger than you, that's why it's 'a'!"

And perhaps that's as good a reason as any that "a" is "a."

Happily, we haven't had to explain it to the kids because, while perhaps they could not understand historically why "a" is "a," they do know that we are bigger than they, and this reason they would feel to be sufficient.

At any rate, they have managed to learn these twenty-six visual abstractions and, what is more, twenty-six auditory abstractions to go with them.

This does not add up to fifty-two possible combinations of sound and picture but instead an almost infinite number of possible combinations.

All this they learn even though we usually teach them at five or six, when it's getting a lot harder for them to learn.

Thank goodness we are wise enough not to try to start law students, medical students, or engineering students with any such wild abstractions, because, being young grownups, they would never survive it.

What your youngster has managed in the first step, *visual differentiation,* is very important.

Reading letters is difficult, since nobody ever ate an *a* or caught an *a* or wore an *a* or opened an *a*. One can eat a *banana,* catch a *ball,* wear a *shirt* or open a *book*. While the letters that make up the word "ball" are abstract, the ball itself is not and thus it is easier to learn the word "ball" than it is to learn the letter *b*.

These two facts make words much easier to read than letters.

The letters of the alphabet are *not* the units of

reading and writing any more than isolated sounds are the units of hearing and speaking. *Words* are the units of language. Letters are simply technical construction materials within words as clay, wood and rock are construction materials of a building. It is the bricks, boards and stones which are the true units of house construction.

Much later, when the child reads well, we will teach him the alphabet. By that time he will be able to see why it was necessary for humans to invent an alphabet and why we need letters.

We begin teaching a small child to read words by using the "self" words because the child learns first about his own body. His world begins inside and works gradually outside, a fact which educators have known for a long time.

A number of years ago a bright child developmentalist expressed by some magic letters something which did much to improve education. These letters are V.A.T.—visual, auditory and tactile. He pointed out that children learn through a combination of seeing (V), hearing (A), and feeling (T). And yet, mothers have always been playing and saying things like, "This little piggy went to market and this little piggy stayed home...," holding the toes up so the child could see them (visual), saying the words so the child could hear them (auditory), and squeezing the toes so the child could feel them (tactile).

In any event, we are now ready for the "self" words.

Parts of the body

hand	hair	leg	shoulder
knee	toes	eye	bellybutton
foot	ear	mouth	finger
head	arm	elbow	teeth
nose	thumb	lips	tongue

You would now add two more sets of words to equal five sets of words in all, or twenty-five words divided into five sets. These two new sets should be taken from the "self" vocabulary.

Here is the method you should use from this point on in adding new words and taking out old ones.

Simply remove one word from each set that has already been taught for five days and replace the word with a new one in each set. Your child's first three sets have already been seen for a week so you may now begin to take out an old word in each set and put in a new one. Five days from now, retire an old word from each of the five sets you are presently using and add a new word to each set. Do this every day.

Mothers find that if they write the date in pencil on the back of the reading card then they can easily tell which words have been shown longest and are ready to be retired.

In summary then, you will be teaching twenty-five words daily, divided into five sets of five words each. Your child will be seeing five new words daily or one in each set, and five words will be retired each day.

Avoid presenting consecutively two words that begin with the same letter. "Hair," "hand" and "head" all begin with "h" and therefore should not be taught consecutively. Occasionally a child will leap to the conclusion that hair is hand because both begin with "h" and are similar in appearance. Children who have already been taught the entire alphabet are much more likely to commit this error than children who do not know the alphabet. Knowing the alphabet causes minor confusion to the child. In teaching the word "arm," for example, mothers may experience the problem of a child's recognizing his old friend *a* and exclaiming over it, instead of reading the word *arm*.

Again, one must remember the supreme rule of never boring the child. If he is bored there is a strong likelihood that you are going too slowly. He should be learning quickly and pushing you to play the game some more.

If you have done it well he will be averaging five new words daily. He may average ten new words a day. If you are clever enough and enthusiastic enough, he may learn more.

When your child has learned the "self" words, you are ready to move to the next step in the process of reading. He now has *two* of the most difficult steps in learning to read behind him. If he has succeeded up to now, you will find it difficult to prevent him from reading much longer.

By now both parent and child should be approaching this game of reading with great pleasure and anticipation. Remember, you are building into your child a love of learning that will multiply throughout his life. More accurately, you are reinforcing a built-in rage for learning which will not be denied, but which can certainly be twisted into useless or even negative channels in a child. Play the game with joy and enthusiasm. Now you are ready to add nouns which are the familiar objects in your child's environment.

The "home" vocabulary consists of those words that name the objects around him, such as "chair" and "wall."

The "home" vocabulary is actually divided

into several sub-vocabularies. These are objects, possessions, foods, animals and "doing" groups.

By this time the child will have a reading vocabulary of twenty-five to thirty words. At this point there is sometimes the temptation to review old words over and over again. Resist this temptation. Your child will find this boring. Children love to learn new words but they do not love to go over and over old ones. You may also be tempted to test your child. Again, do not do this. Testing invariably introduces tension into the situation on the part of the parent, and children perceive this readily. They are likely to associate tension and unpleasantness with learning.

Be sure to show your child how much you love and respect him at every opportunity.

Objects

chair	table	door
window	wall	bed
bathtub	stove	refrigerator
television	sofa	toilet

This list should also be added to or subtracted from to reflect the child's home surrounding and family-owned items which are special to his particular family.

Now continue to feed your child's happy hunger with the possessions words.

Possessions (things that belong to the child himself)

truck	blanket	socks
cup	spoon	pajamas
shoes	ball	tricycle
toothbrush	pillow	bottle

Foods

juice	milk	orange
bread	water	carrot
butter	egg	apple
banana	potato	strawberry

Animals

elephant	**giraffe**	**hippopotamus**
whale	**gorilla**	**dinosaur**
rhinoceros	**spider**	**dog**
tiger	**snake**	**fox**

As in the previous sub-vocabularies, these lists should be altered to reflect your child's own particular possessions and those things he or she loves the most. Obviously, the list will vary somewhat depending upon whether your child is twelve months old or whether he is five years old.

Your child is taught the words in exactly the same way he has been taught up to now. This list can vary from ten words to fifty words, as the parent and the child choose.

The reading list (which up to this point may be approximately fifty words) has been composed entirely of nouns. The next grouping in the home vocabulary reflects action and consequently introduces verbs.

Actions

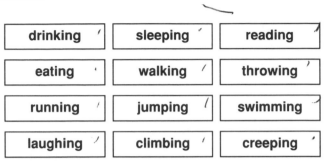

drinking	sleeping	reading
eating	walking	throwing
running	jumping	swimming
laughing	climbing	creeping

For added fun with this set, as each new word is taught mother first illustrates the act by (for example), jumping, and saying, "Mommy is jumping." She then has the child jump and says, "You are jumping." Mother now shows her child the word and says, "This word says 'jumping.'" In this way she goes through all the "action" words. The child will particularly enjoy this, since it involves him, his mother (or father), action and learning.

When your child has learned the basic "home" words he is ready to move ahead.

By now your child is reading more than fifty words and both you and he should be delighted. Two points should be made before continuing to the next step, which is the beginning of the end in the process of learning to read.

If the parent has approached teaching his or her child to read as sheer pleasure (as should ideally be the case) rather than as a duty or obligation (which in the end is not a good enough reason), then both the parent and child should be enjoying themselves immensely in the daily sessions.

John Ciardi, in the editorial which has already been mentioned, said of the child, "if he has been loved (which is basically to say, if he has been played with by parents who found honest pleasure in the play). . . ." This is a superb description of love—play *and* learning with a child—and it should never be far from a parent's mind while teaching a child to read.

The next point for a parent to remember is that children are vastly curious about words, whether written or spoken. When a child expresses interest in a word, for whatever reason, it is now wise to print it for him and add it to his vocabulary. He will learn quickly and easily any word that he has asked about.

Therefore, if a child should ask, "Mommy, what is a rhinoceros?" or "What does microscopic mean?" it is wise to answer the question carefully and then print the word immediately, and so add it to his reading vocabulary.

He will feel a special pride and get additional pleasure from learning to read words which he himself generated.

S T E P T W O *(Couplets and phrases)*

Once a child has acquired a basic reading vocabulary of single words, he is now reading to
put those words together to make couplets (two
word combinations) and phrases (more than
two word combinations).

This is an important intermediate step between single words and whole sentences.
Couplets and phrases create a bridge between
the basic building blocks of reading—single
words—and the next unit of organization—the
sentence. Of course the ability to read a whole
group of related words called a sentence is the
next large objective. However, this intermediate
step of couplets and short phrases will help the
child progress by easy steps to this next level.

Now mother reviews her child's vocabulary
and determines what couplets she can make
using the words she has already taught. She will
quickly discover that she needs some modifying
words in her child's diet in order to make couplets and short phrases that make sense.

One simple group of words which are very
helpful and easy to teach are basic colors:

red	violet	blue
orange	black	pink
yellow	white	gray
green	brown	purple

These words can be made with squares of the appropriate color on the back of each card. Mother can then teach the reading word and flip the card over to reveal the color itself.

Very young children learn colors quickly and easily and take great delight in pointing out colors wherever they go. After the basic colors have been taught, there is a whole world of more subtle shades to be explored (indigo, azure, chartreuse, olive, gold, silver, copper, etc.)

Once these simple colors have been introduced, mother can make her child's first set of couplets:

orange juice	**pink toes**
blue eyes	**violet grapes**
red truck	**brown hair**
yellow banana	**green apple**
black shoe	**white refrigerator**

Each of these couplets has the great virtue that the child knows both words as a single word. The couplet contains two basic elements that are satisfying to the child. One aspect he enjoys is seeing old words he already knows. The second element is that although he already knows these two words he now sees that his two old words combined create a new idea. This is exciting to him. It opens the door on understanding the magic of the printed page.

As mother progresses with this step she will feel the need of additional modifiers. These will best be taught in pairs as opposites:

big	little	long	short
fat	thin	right	left
clean	dirty	happy	sad
smooth	rough	empty	full
pretty	ugly	dark	light

Again, depending on the age and experience of the child, you may or may not need to introduce these cards with a picture on the back of the card to illustrate the idea. "Big" and "little" are simple ideas for a very young child. What little child does not instantly recognize when his older brother or sister has been given something "bigger" than he has received? We adults are apt to view these ideas as abstractions, and they are, but these ideas surround the young child and he grasps them quickly when they are presented in a logical and straightforward manner. These ideas are closely related to his day-to-day survival so they are, in a manner of speaking, close to his heart.

We can now present couplets:

empty cup	full cup
big chair	little chair
happy Mommy	sad Mommy
long hair	short hair
clean shirt	dirty shirt
right hand	left hand

STEP THREE (*Phrases*)

It is a simple step to hop from couplets to phrases. When we do, the leap is made by adding action to the couplets and creating a basic short sentence.

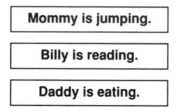

Even with a basic vocabulary of fifty to seventy-five words the possible combinations are many. There are three excellent ways to teach simple phrases and a wise mother will use not one, but all three.

1. Using the single reading cards you have already made, make some "is" cards. Sit down with five names of people or animals, five "is" cards and five "actions." Choose one of each and put together a phrase. Read it to your child. Now let your child choose one of each group and make a phrase. Read his phrase to him. Together make three to five phrases. Then put the cards away. You can play this game as often as your child likes. Remember to change the nouns and verbs often to keep the game fresh.

Mommy	**is**	**eating**
Daddy	**is**	**sleeping**
Sally	**is**	**laughing**
Jimmy	**is**	**running**
Amy	**is**	**climbing**

Mother's choice

Sally	is	climbing

Child's choice

Jimmy	is	running

2. Using your 4" by 24" poster board cards, make a set of five phrases. You will have to decrease your print size in order to fit three or four words onto the cards. Now make your letters 2" high rather than 3." As you do this be sure not to crowd the words. Leave enough white space so each word can "breathe." Show them three times daily for five days (or less). Then add two *new* phrases daily and retire two old ones daily. Your child will learn these very quickly so be willing to move on to new phrases as quickly as possible.

The elephant is eating

3. Make a simple phrase book. This book should have five phrases with a simple illustration for each phrase. The book should be 8" by 18" with 2" red lettering. The printed

page precedes and is separated from the illustration. It is wise to make the first such book a simple diary of your child's day.

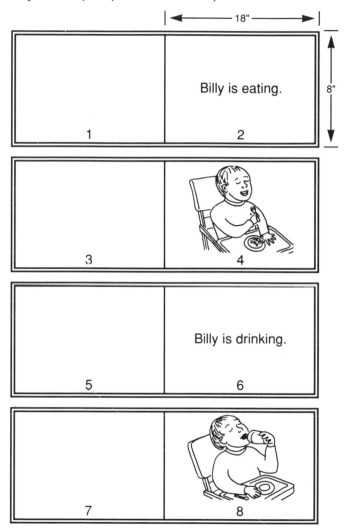

His new book can easily be illustrated using photographs of your child doing each of these things. This little book becomes the first in a long series of books that trace the growth and development and the life and times of your child.

These books are naturally loved by every child lucky enough to have a mother who takes the time to make them. Each book starts out as a modest little ten-page book that mother reads to her child two to three times daily for a few days. Then mother introduces a new chapter which uses the same basic vocabulary.

These wonderful little homemade diaries of your child's life are a living, breathing way to use all the great photographs that every mother has taken of her child over the years.

S T E P   F O U R   (*Sentences*)

In truth the simple phrases we have just discussed are also short sentences. But now the child is ready for the most important step after being able to differentiate single words. Now he is ready to tackle full sentences that express a more complete thought.

If we could understand only sentences that we had seen and known before, our reading would indeed be limited. All of the anticipation in opening a new book lies in finding what the book is going to say that we have never read before.

To recognize individual words and to realize that they represent an object or an idea is a basic step in learning to read. To recognize that words, when used in a sentence, can represent a more complicated idea is an additional and vitally important step.

We now can use the same basic procedures introduced when we began phrases. However we now go beyond three words. Instead of choosing from five nouns and five verbs to make the simple phrase "Mommy is eating," now we add five objects and present "Mommy is eating a banana."

Again we need a group of "a," "an" or "the" cards. These should not be taught separately since the child will learn them in the context of the sentence where they serve a purpose and make sense; outside the context they are of little interest to the child.

While he uses the word "the" correctly in ordinary speech and therefore understands it, he does not deal with it as an isolated word. It is, of course, vital to reading that he *recognize* and *read* it as a separate word, but it is not necessary that he be able to define it. In the same way, all children speak correctly long before they know the rules of grammar. Besides, how would you like to explain what "the" means, even to a ten-year-old? So don't. Just be sure he can read it.

When you have made four-word sentences using the three methods described in the third step (phrases) then you can add modifiers—adjectives and adverbs—that give life to a proper sentence:

Mommy is eating a yellow banana.

Again, as you add additional words you will need to decrease the print size a little bit. Now decrease the size of your letters to 1 1/2". Give each word plenty of room or, if needed, make cards longer than eighteen inches.

If you have been playing the game of making sentences with your child consistently, you will already have noticed that your child delights in making sentences that are ridiculous or absurd.

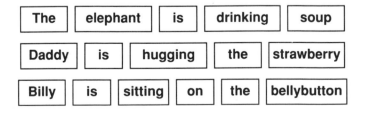

This should inspire you to do the same. It is a sad commentary that our formal education was so drab and sterile that without realizing it we avoid using humor and absurdity in our teaching. We were so often reminded not to "be silly" or "act ridiculous" that we assume it is against the law to have fun when one is teaching or learning. This notion is the very soul of absurdity, for fun *is* learning and learning *is* fun. *The more fun going on, the more learning is taking place.*

A good sentence-making session usually finds mother and child trying to outdo each other in creating riotous combinations and ends with a lot of noisy tickling, hugging, and merriment.

Since every sentence you are creating or putting on cards or in books is composed of single words that you have already carefully taught beforehand, it is probable that your child will go through many sentences very quickly.

You are wise to take a limited vocabulary of perhaps fifty words and use them to make as many sentences as you and your child can create. In this way your child will really strengthen his mastery of these words. His confidence will grow so that no matter what combination or permutation is presented in a new sentence, he will be able to decode it.

At this stage you are still presenting this material to him. You are reading the sentences or books aloud to him. Depending on his age, language ability, or personality, he may be actually saying some words aloud spontaneously or reading whole sentences aloud. If he does this spontaneously that is fine. However you should not ask him to read aloud to you. We will discuss this point at length later in the next chapter.

As you go from four-word sentences to five-word sentences and longer you will no doubt begin to run out of space on the 4" by 24" cards or 8" by 18" books.

Now by *evolution* you are going to do three things.

1. Reduce the print size;
2. Increase the number of words;
3. Change the print from red to black.

Begin by reducing print size a little bit. You do not want to reduce it so much that your child has the slightest difficulty with it. Try 1" print. Use this for several weeks. If this does not appear to be a problem, then you are ready to increase the number of words. If you have been using five-word sentences, now go to six-word sentences. However, leave the print size at 1" Now continue with six-word sentences for a while. If all goes well, then reduce your print size to 7/8".

The important rule to observe in this process is never to reduce print size and increase the number of words at the same time.

First reduce print size slightly and live with it for a while, then increase the number of words.

Do both of these things gradually. Remember, the sentence cannot be too big or too clear, but it could be too small or too confusing. You never want to rush this process.

If you do reduce the print size too quickly or increase the number of words too fast you will notice your child's attention and interest dropping. He might begin to look away from the printed matter altogether and simply look at you because the card or page is visually too complex for him. If this should occur, simply return to the print size or number of words you were using *right before* this happened and his enthusiasm will return. Stay at this level for a good while longer before attempting to change things again.

You do not really need to change the size or color of single words. In fact we have found that keeping single words large is easier for both mother and child.

However, when you are making books with one inch letters or six words or more on a page, we recommend changing from red to black print. As words get smaller, black does provide better contrast and a more legible page.

Now the stage has been set for the final and most exciting step of all—the book. We have already gotten our foot solidly in the door by creating many little couplet books, phrase books, and sentence books, but if these steps are the skeleton, it is the next one that is the meat.

The path has been cleared, so let's get to it.

S T E P   F I V E   (*Books*)

Now your child is ready to read a real and proper book. In fact he has already read many homemade books and completed all the single words, couplets, and phrases that he will find in his first book.

The careful preparation that has gone before is the key to his success in his first book and indeed for many books to come.

His ability to handle very large-print single words, couplets, phrases and sentences has been established. But now he must be able to handle smaller print and a greater number of words on each page.

The younger a child is, the more challenging this step will be. Remember that as you have taught him to read, you have actually been growing his visual pathway, exactly as exercise grows the biceps.

In the event you are reducing the print size too quickly and therefore presenting print that your child is not yet capable of reading easily, you will have a clear indication of what print size *is* easy and comfortable for your child from doing the *third* and *fourth steps* of your program.

Since the words he is using are exactly the same words but differ only in the fact that they become smaller with each step, you can now see quite clearly if a child is learning faster than his visual pathway is able to mature.

As an example, suppose that a child completes the *third* and *fourth steps* successfully with 2" words but has difficulty in reading the identical words in the book itself. The answer is simple. The words are too small. We know that the child can read 2" words easily. Now the parent simply prepares additional words and simple sentences 2" in height. Use simple, imaginative words and sentences that the child will enjoy reading. After two months of this, return again to the book with its smaller print.

Remember that if the print were made too small *you* would also have trouble reading it.

If the child is three years of age by the time you get to the 7/8" print of the book itself, you will probably not be held up at all at this point. If the child is less than two years old by the time you get to the book, it is almost certain that you will need to obtain or create additional books with 1" or 2" print for the child. Fine; it is all reading, and real reading at that. It will mature his brain growth far more than would otherwise be the case.

The parent will now need to procure the book which he will teach his child to read. Find a book which contains vocabulary that you have already taught as single words, couplets and phrases. The choice of the book to be used is very important; it should meet the following standards:

1. It should have a vocabulary of fifty to one hundred words;
2. It should present no more than one sentence on a single page;
3. The printing should be no less than 7/8" high;
4. Text should precede and be separated from illustrations.

Unfortunately, at present, few commercial books meet all of these requirements. Examples of books created for the Better Baby Press with these requirements in mind are:

1. *Enough, Inigo, Enough;*
2. *Inigo McKenzie, The Contrary Man;*
3. *You Can't Stay a Baby Forever;*
4. *NOSE Is Not TOES.*

However, one or two books will hardly be enough to keep your eager young reader fed and happy—you will need *many*. Therefore, the simplest means of providing your child with proper books at this stage is to buy interesting and well-written commercial books and make them over with the large, clear printed pages your young child requires. You can then cut out the professional illustrations and include them in the book you are making.

Sometimes it will be necessary to simplify the text to suit your child's reading. Or you may find books with beautiful illustrations but silly or repetitive text that would bore your child. In this case rewrite the text using more sophisticated vocabulary and more mature sentence structure.

The content of the book is vital. Your child will want to read a book for exactly the same reasons that we adults read books. He will expect to be entertained or given new information—preferably both. He will enjoy well-written adventure stories, fairy tales and mysteries. There is a world of wonderful fiction already written and waiting to be written. He will also enjoy nonfiction. Books that teach him about the lives of famous people or animals are vastly popular with tiny children.

Perhaps the easiest rule to follow is, do you find the book interesting? If not, the chances are excellent your three-year-old won't find much to interest him either.

It is far, far better to aim a bit over his head and let him reach upward than to run the risk of boring him with pap and pablum.

Remember the following rules:

1. Create or choose books that will be interesting to your child;
2. Introduce all new vocabulary as single words before beginning the book;
3. Make the text large and clear;
4. Make sure your child has to turn the page to see the illustration that follows the text.

Once you have completed the above steps, you are ready to begin the book with your child.

Sit down with him and read the book to him. He may want to read some of the words instead of having you do it. If he does this spontaneously, fine. This will depend largely on his age and personality. The younger a child is, the less he will wish to read aloud. In this case you read and he will follow along.

Read at a natural speed, with enthusiasm and a lot of expression in your voice. It is not necessary to point to each word as you read. However, your child may wish to do so. If he does, this is fine, as long as you do not slow down.

Read the book two to three times daily for several days. Each book will have its own life. Some books are ready for the shelf in a few days, others are demanded daily for weeks.

Your child now begins his own library of books. Once you have retired a book, it goes on his shelf. He may then read it himself as many times a day as he likes.

As this little library of superb custom-made books grows, it is the source of much pleasure and pride to the tiny child. At this stage he will probably begin taking one of his books with him wherever he goes.

While other children are bored driving in the car, waiting in line at the supermarket, or sitting in a restaurant, your little fellow has his books—his old books, which he cherishes and reads again and again and his new books, which he looks forward to every week.

At this point it is impossible to provide too many books. He will devour them. The more he gets the more he wants. In a world where 30 percent of the eighteen-year-olds in our school system will not be able to read in a useful way and many will graduate unable to read their own high school diplomas or labels on jars, this problem of keeping the young child supplied with books is the right problem to have.

Summary

There are three distinct levels of understanding in the process of learning how to read. As the child conquers each of them he will show exuberance at his new and very exciting discovery. The joy Columbus must have known in finding a new world could hardly have been greater than that which the child will experience at each of these levels.

Naturally, his first pleasure and delight is in the disclosure that words have meaning. To the child this is almost like a secret code that he shares with grownups. He will enjoy this vastly and visibly.

Next he notices that the words he reads can be used together and are therefore more than merely labels for objects. This is also a new and wonderful revelation.

The last discovery he makes will probably be very noticeable to the parent. This, the greatest of them all, is that the book he is reading represents more than the simple fun of translating secret names into objects, and more even than the decoding of strings of words into comments about objects and people. Suddenly and delightfully the big secret bursts upon the child that this book is actually talking to him, and to him alone. When the child comes to this realization (and this does not necessarily happen until he has read many books), there will be no stopping him. He will now be a reader in every sense of the word. He now realizes that the words he already knows can be rearranged to make entirely new ideas. He does not have to learn a new set of words every time he has to read something.

What a discovery this is! Few things will compare to it in later life. He can now have an adult talking to him in a new conversation any time he wants, simply by picking up a new book.

All of man's knowledge is now available to him. Not only the knowledge of people he knows in his home and neighborhood, but people far away whom he will never see. Even more than that, he can be approached by people who lived long ago in other places and in other ages.

The power to control our own fate began, as we shall see, with our ability to write and to read. Because humans have been able to write and to read, they have been able to pass on to other humans centuries later and in remote places the knowledge they have gained. Human knowledge is cumulative.

Humans are human essentially because they can read and write.

This is the true importance of what your child discovers when he learns to read. The child may even try in his own way to tell you about his great discovery, lest you, his parent, miss it. If he does, listen to him respectfully and with love. What he has to say is important.

18

how to give your baby encyclopedic knowledge

The acquisition of knowledge is, in an intellectual sense, the objective of life. It is knowledge from which all else springs—science, art, music, language, literature and all that matters to humans.

Knowledge is based on information and information can be gained only through facts. Each fact is a single bit of information. When such a fact is presented to a child in a proper way, it becomes a *Bit of Intelligence,* both in the sense that it literally grows his brain, and in the sense that it is the base of all his future knowledge.

This chapter will take the parent and the child through the Encyclopedic Knowledge Program and thus lead the way to all knowledge.

Parents wishing to have more information about the principles of giving their babies encyclopedic knowledge are advised to read the book *How To Give Your Baby Encyclopedic Knowledge.*

This chapter is written as if it were addressed to full-time professional mothers so that there will be no limits to what the parent who actually is a professional mother can do.

It should in no way intimidate the mother who is not with her baby full time. This mother simply teaches a smaller number of categories.

Isn't it wonderful that there is more to learn than we can learn in a lifetime?

The program of encyclopedic knowledge should be begun when you have started your reading program and feel comfortable with it. This may be a few weeks after you have begun the reading program or it may be several months. These two programs complement each other greatly.

The reading program is clearly the most

important of all. This program, like the reading program, is also a tremendous amount of fun and will provide a child with the most pleasure throughout life, encompassing, as it does, science, art, music, history and all the other bewitching things life has to offer.

What is a "Bit of Intelligence" card?

A "*Bit of Intelligence*" card represents one bit of information. A *Bit of Intelligence* card is made using an accurate drawing or illustration or excellent quality photograph. It has certain important characteristics. It must be precise, discrete, non-ambiguous and new. It must also be large and clear. It should not be called a "flash card," which tends to degrade it.

PRECISE
By precise we mean accurate, with appropriate detail. It should be as exact as we can humanly make it.

If the *Bit of Intelligence* card is made with a drawing of a crow, it must be very carefully and clearly drawn.

DISCRETE
By discrete we mean one item. There should only be one subject on a *Bit of Intelligence* card.

If the *Bit of Intelligence* card is made with a drawing of a crow, it must not also have in it a cow, a mountain, a flower and some clouds.

NON-AMBIGUOUS

By non-ambiguous we mean named specifically, with a certainty of meaning. Therefore each *Bit of Intelligence* card carries a label that can be interpreted in only one way.

If it is a crow, it must be labelled **Crow** and not "a large black bird."

NEW

By new we mean something your child does not already know.

The drawing which follows illustrates an incorrect image for a *Bit of Intelligence* card. The drawing is imprecise because the crow shown has no detail and merges with the other crow in the background.

It is not discrete because there are two crows, mountains, a twig with leaves and some clouds all in the same picture.

It would be ambiguous even if labelled **Crow** because of the number of subjects in the picture.

Unacceptable image for "Crow " *Bit of Intelligence* card

The next drawing illustrates a correct image for a *Bit of Intelligence* card. The drawing is precise because the crow shown is detailed and clearly drawn.

It is discrete because there is only one subject represented.

It is non-ambiguous because there can be no question that it is a crow and would be correctly labelled as such on the reverse side of the card.

Good image for "Crow " *Bit of Intelligence* card

Therefore any proposed piece of visual information, to be truly appropriate for a *Bit of Intelligence* card for your child, must pass six tests.

1. It must have accurate detail;
2. It must be one item only;
3. It must be specifically named;
4. It must be new;
5. It must be large;
6. It must be clear.

If any one of those characteristics is missing, the *Bit of Intelligence* card should not be included in your Encyclopedic Knowledge Program.

If all those characteristics are present, then it is an appropriate *Bit of Intelligence* card and will be easily learned by your child when done as part of this program.

Please make sure that you understand completely what is correct for a *Bit of Intelligence* card before beginning to put together and organize your program.

How to Find Images for Bit of Intelligence *Cards*

Mothers have made literally hundreds of thousands of *Bit of Intelligence* cards for their children at home. The best sources of images are books, magazines, maps, posters, teaching cards and museum cards.

The best type of books are all-color "Treasury of (subject)" books. Treasuries of birds, flowers, insects and mammals are excellent sources for categories of visual material. The purpose of these books is to instruct and inform and the quality of the illustrations and photographs is generally very good. This type of book provides you with a category all ready to go.

Magazines can also be a valuable source of

pictures for *Bit of Intelligence* cards. However, not just any magazine will do. If you are interested in teaching about wildlife, then the wide variety of wildlife magazines will provide you with valuable photos and drawings.

Maps of counties, states, countries and continents have proved invaluable for making geography *Bit of Intelligence* cards. Since many other categories can be related to geography, maps have become a source used by our mothers.

Posters of all kinds provide excellent raw materials for *Bit of Intelligence* cards. Governmental agencies often have posters on regional information that can be made into fine teaching materials.

Almost all museums offer some good raw materials for *Bit of Intelligence* cards. Reproductions of famous artists' works, sculpture and architecture are readily available. Science museums are also a potential source for photos, drawings and diagrams.

The Better Baby Press pioneered and publishes *Bit of Intelligence* cards and makes these materials available to the public.

There are no limits to what can be found that is food for your baby's brain, heart and soul other than your own ingenuity and the limits of human knowledge.

How to Prepare Bit of Intelligence *Cards*

QUALITY

It is not difficult to make fine quality *Bit of Intelligence* cards at home. Indeed the quality must be fine in order for you to use these precious materials with your even more precious child. You should prepare your materials with one thing foremost in your mind—quality.

This is not a cute game you will be playing with your child, nor icing on the cake. It is his introduction to the knowledge of the world.

Your *Bit of Intelligence* cards should reflect your respect for what you are going to teach and what your child is going to learn. There is no more precious commodity than knowledge. The only thing worse than something cheap wrapped up in finery is something beyond value made up cheaply.

Your *Bit of Intelligence* cards should be regarded as family heirlooms destined to be handed down tenderly from one child to the next, then jealously guarded and saved for the grandchildren.

MATERIALS

You will need the following materials which are usually readily available.

1. Photos, drawings and other visual material appropriate for making *Bit of Intelligence* cards;
2. Poster board;
3. Black *Magic Marker* or other waterproof felt-tipped marker;
4. Rubber cement;
5. Clear *Contact Paper* or laminate (optional).

APPROPRIATE VISUAL MATERIAL FOR MAKING *BIT OF INTELLIGENCE* CARDS

Again, you will want photos, drawings and other visual material that is precise, discrete, non-ambiguous and new. Your raw materials for making *Bit of Intelligence* cards must be precise and new when you get them. However materials which are not discrete or non-ambiguous can often be made so after you have found them.

You will quickly become expert at deciding whether a picture has potential or not. If you have a good potential image for a *Bit of Intelligence* card but it has a distracting background, simply cut around the subject and eliminate the background.

If there is a group of objects within the picture, cut each out individually and make each into a *Bit of Intelligence* card.

If the raw material has writing underneath it or around it, cut this away.

If the subject has a vague, ambiguous or misleading title make sure you have the clearest and most complete label you can find. For example, "turtle" is hardly informative. You need to be specific with **Ornate Box Turtle**.

Finally, before you throw the left-over material away, make sure you have saved and filed any information that came along with the subject you have selected. You are going to be needing that information in the future for your child, so put it where you can find it easily some months later.

POSTER BOARD

We recommend that *Bit of Intelligence* cards be made using white, two-sided, cardboard. This is sometimes referred to as "poster board," "index board," "illustration board," etc., depending on the composition and quality of the material.

Paper does not have adequate rigidity to be used for *Bit of Intelligence* cards.

The cardboard you use should be able to be held in one hand and not "flop" and should be strong enough to hold up under repeated handling (especially if you plan to have babies beyond those you are currently teaching).

Where white cardboard does not provide adequate contrast with the subject of the *Bit of Intelligence* card being prepared, use black poster board or an appropriate color for contrast.

To make your job easier, have your cardboard pre-cut. If you are buying from a stationery store, art supply store or paper supply dealer, have them do the work for you with their heavy paper-cutter. Cardboard size should be 11" x 11" (28 cm. x 28 cm).

BLACK WATERPROOF MARKER

To letter the reverse side of your *Bit of Intelligence* cards you will need a wide-tipped black marker. These are marketed under a variety of brand names, one of the most popular being *Magic Marker.* This type of marker is waterproof and uses a varnish base ink. Be careful to replace the tops of your markers when not in use so that the varnish base does not evaporate. Also keep these tools out of your child's reach.

RUBBER CEMENT

We have found that rubber cement is the best vehicle for fixing photos and drawings to cardboard. Apply a thin coat of rubber cement to the back of the picture and to the approximate area of the cardboard where the picture will be situated. When both surfaces are sufficiently dry, press the picture to the cardboard. The bond can be strengthened by placing a clean sheet of paper over your new *Bit of Intelligence* card and rubbing your hand across the surface.

LAMINATION

The ideal *Bit of Intelligence* card has clear plastic laminate on both sides. Lamination strengthens the card, making it more difficult to damage, as well as making it resistant to fingerprints and soil. When you consider the time and attention you put into making each *Bit of Intelligence* card, it seems logical that you would wish to preserve it in the best possible way for your future use or the use of others in your family.

Most families cannot afford to have their *Bit of Intelligence* cards laminated by machine. However, it is possible to purchase wide rolls of clear *Contact Paper* which is a self-adhering, easy-to-use material. It is available in hardware and paint stores that sell kitchen and drawer shelf paper.

PUTTING IT ALL TOGETHER

You have now assembled all the materials that you need to make beautiful *Bit of Intelligence* cards. Now set up a production line so that you get the most out of what you have found.

First, prepare the raw visual material that you

have, being sure that you have the correct identification of each item, and that you have filed any pertinent information about the item.

Second, if the item itself is not discrete, cut out the background so that you have only one item mounted on the card.

Third (and this step is often missed by the novice *Bit of Intelligence* card-maker, to her immediate chagrin), label the reverse side of the cardboard before mounting the image, preventing your needing to throw out the entire thing if you make a mistake while labeling. Proper identification of the item should be neatly lettered on the reverse side, using a wide-tipped permanent black marker. Letter size should be no less than one inch high—actually, the larger the better.

$$\boxed{\text{\textbf{Crow}}}$$

Next, with your cardboard labelled, glue your prepared raw material using rubber cement. Be careful to use a thin coat of rubber cement, especially if the raw image has printing on its reverse side. Generous coats of rubber cement may cause ink to bleed through once the image is mounted, ruining a careful job.

You now have a high-quality, sturdy teaching tool. If you wish to preserve it for many years, you may take the additional step of laminating your new *Bit of Intelligence* card as described above.

ORGANIZATION

Bit of Intelligence cards are always organized into categories. You will find that your categories start out being very broad. For example—ten typical beginning categories are birds, presidents of the United States, states of the United States, musical symbols, paintings of Van Gogh, bones of the body, dots, simple tools, Japanese body words and American writers.

A look at the same program eighteen months later will show a great increase in the sophistication of the organization of *Bit of Intelligence* cards. Birds are now water fowl, seed-eaters and scavengers. In short, you will be constantly arranging and rearranging the overall organization of your *Bit of Intelligence* card library to reflect your child's growing ability to connect and relate one category to another.

Each category should have a minimum of ten *Bit of Intelligence* cards and there is no limit to the number a category may ultimately have.

This depends entirely on availability and your child's interest and enthusiasm for that category.

When you are finished actively using a *Bit of Intelligence* card, you should carefully file it, according to category, so that you can retrieve it for later use.

SUMMARY

1. Know the full criteria for a *Bit of Intelligence* card.
2. Find a wide variety of raw material for *Bit of Intelligence* cards.
3. Organize the raw material into categories.
4. Cut out subjects for your *Bit of Intelligence* cards.
5. Save information about those subjects for future Programs of Intelligence.
6. Cut or obtain 11" x 11" white poster board.
7. Label 11" x 11" card on back with a black marker.
8. Put rubber cement on the image to be used on the *Bit of Intelligence* card.
9. Mount the image on the front of the 11" x 11" card.
10. Put clear *Contact Paper* or laminate on finished *Bit of Intelligence* card (optional).
11. Create a workable filing system for retired *Bit of Intelligence* cards.

Categories of Bit of Intelligence *Cards*

It is clear from the criteria for a *Bit of Intelligence* card that any piece of new information that can be presented precisely, discretely and non-ambiguously is the basic building block of intelligence. The mortar that holds that structure together is the categorization of *Bit of Intelligence* cards.

A category is a group of ten or more *Bit of Intelligence* cards which are directly related to each other. For example *Birds* are a category.

BIRDS

1. **Common Crow**
2. **Robin**
3. **Bluejay**
4. **Mockingbird**
5. **Cardinal Grosbeak**
6. **Ring-necked Pheasant**
7. **Bald Eagle**
8. **Wood Duck**
9. **House Sparrow**
10. **Pileated Woodpecker.**

This category of birds may be expanded to include every bird that ever lived, from prehistoric birds up to the present, or it may stop after thirty birds. In short, a category contains no fewer than ten *Bit of Intelligence* cards and is limited in breadth only by the number of species or members that exist in that group.

For example, the category of presidents of the United States will only expand as new presidents are elected.

Why Related Bit of Intelligence *Cards?*

This seemingly simple organizational detail has a profoundly important effect on the tiny child. If we present a tiny child with ten unrelated *Bit of Intelligence* cards which are each precise, discrete, non-ambiguous and new we have given him ten superb pieces of knowledge. That is a marvelous thing to do. He will have these ten facts forever.

If you do it correctly you can show those ten cards to a tiny baby in ten seconds. Taking thirty seconds is far too slow to keep his attention.

That's a wonderful thing to do and when you use ten seconds in such a way three or four times he will have the information cold and for the rest of his life if you review it now and then.

But in the same ten seconds we can give him ten *related Bit of Intelligence* cards which will give him a minimum of 3,628,800 permutations and combinations, which is an even more powerful use of ten seconds, and this is why we use *Bit of Intelligence* cards in categories.

We call these related *Bit of Intelligence* card subjects Categories of Intelligence.

Choosing Categories

We have chosen to divide all existing knowledge into ten divisions.

1. Biology
2. History
3. Geography
4. Music
5. Art
6. Mathematics
7. Human Physiology
8. General Science
9. Language
10. Literature

Obviously we could have placed all information in five divisions, or a hundred. Why we have chosen these divisions will become clear as we proceed.

It should be your objective to give your child the broadest foundation of knowledge that you can provide. You would be wise to choose one category from each of the ten divisions of knowledge above when you begin. Here are some examples:

Division: *Biology*
Category: *Birds*
***Bit of Intelligence* cards**:
Mockingbird   *Ring-necked Pheasant*
Bluejay   *Common Crow*
Cardinal Grosbeak   *Bald Eagle*
Wood Duck   *House Sparrow*
Pileated Woodpecker *Robin, etc.*
(These are pictures of the birds.)

Division: *History*
Category: *Presidents of the United States*
***Bit of Intelligence* cards:**
George Washington   *John Adams*
Thomas Jefferson   *James Madison*
James Monroe   *John Quincy Adams*
Andrew Jackson   *Martin Van Buren*
William H. Harrison   *John Tyler, etc.*
(These are pictures of the presidents.)

Division: *Geography*
Category: *States of the United States*
***Bit of Intelligence* cards:**

Maine	*Vermont*
Rhode Island	*New Hampshire*
New York	*Massachusetts*
Pennsylvania	*New Jersey*
Delaware	*Maryland, etc.*

(These are outlines of the shapes of the states.)

Division: *Music*
Category: *Musical symbols*
***Bit of Intelligence* cards:**

A   B   C   D   E   F   G
treble clef   bass clef   whole note, etc.
(The musical signs themselves as above.)

Division: *Art*
Category: *Paintings of Van Gogh*
***Bit of Intelligence* cards:**

The School Boy	*Madame Roulin &*
	Her Baby
Sunflowers	*Self-Portrait*
The Postman Roulin	*Gypsy Caravans*
Old Man in Sorrow	*Church at Auvers*
Cafe Terrace at Night	*Field with Peach Trees*
	in Blossom, etc.

(These are reproductions of the paintings.)

Division: *Human Physiology*
Category: *Bones of the Body*
***Bit of Intelligence* cards:**

cranium	*mandible*	*ribs*	*tibia*
radius	*vertebrae*	*fibula*	*ulna*
phalanges	*clavicle, etc.*		

(These are drawings of the bones.)

Division: *Mathematics*
Category: *Pure Quantity (dots)*
***Bit of Intelligence* cards:**

●, ●●, ●●●, ●●●●, ●●●●●, ●●●●●●, ●●●●●●●, ●●●●●●●●, ●●●●●●●●●, ●●●●●●●●●●, etc.

(These are red dots on cards. See Chapter 19 on math.)

Division: *General Science*
Category: *Simple Tools*
***Bit of Intelligence* cards:**

scissors	*knife*	*saw*	*hammer*
axe	*screwdriver*	*drill*	*clamp*
broom	*lever, etc.*		

(These are drawings or photos of the tools.)

Division: *Language*
Category: *Japanese*
***Bit of Intelligence* cards:**

me (eyes)	*mimi* (ears)
oheyso (bellybutton)	*atama* (head)
kata (shoulders)	*hana* (nose)
kuchi (mouth)	*kaminoke* (hair)
ashi (feet)	*hiza* (knee), etc.

(These are printed words on cards. See Chapter 17 on reading.)

Division: *Literature*
Category: *American Writers*
***Bit of Intelligence* cards:**

Thomas Jefferson	*Thomas Paine*
Nathaniel Hawthorne	*Herman Melville*
Edgar Allen Poe	*Louisa May Alcott*
Henry David Thoreau	*F. Scott Fitzgerald*
Ernest Hemingway	*Mark Twain, etc.*

(These are portraits or photos of the writers.)

Your child's intellectual diet should be a broad one. The more categories that are taught, the wider view your child has of the world. It is not our intention to steer our children in one direction or the other—quite the reverse. We wish to offer them a sampler of the whole world. It will then be up to them to decide what directions they wish to take.

When a wide spectrum of categories is offered, these decisions will be made on the basis of broad knowledge rather than on the basis of broad ignorance.

How to Teach Using Bit of Intelligence *Cards*

The following section will assist you in teaching your child with *Bit of Intelligence* cards. Although this technical information is important, the most vital and valuable ingredient in your program is within you. It is the affection and respect with which you teach. This technical information is to help insure that the intimate relationship you and your child share will be continually developing and growing through the teaching process.

ONE SESSION

Choose the first category that you would like to show to your child. That category contains ten *Bit of Intelligence* cards.

Position yourself and your child comfortably facing each other. Hold the cards about 18" away from your child.

Begin by announcing joyously, "I have some birds to show you!"

Then as quickly as your fingers will allow you, move the back card in the stack to the front and say, "This bird is a common crow"; "This bird is a robin"; "This bird is a bluejay".

By taking the back card and moving it to the front you get a quick look at the name on the back of the card you are about to present. Then as you put that card out front you give your child its name.

With great enthusiasm you zoom through these ten cards. Your goal is to do them as fast as you possibly can. This should take 10-15 seconds—certainly no more than that. One second for each card—and five seconds for you to fumble the cards. You'll quickly become skilled at doing this.

For the first few days after introducing a new category you should continue to say, "This bird is a (name)," but after that say only, "common crow," "robin," "bluejay," etc., as fast as you can. Children catch on to the rules very quickly.

It is wise to make sure all your *Bit of Intelligence* cards are right-side-up and turned label side toward you before you begin so that none of your child's time is wasted while you straighten out cards. Also, you should reshuffle the cards after each session so they are not being shown in the same order each time.

As you are aware from teaching your child to read, you need to eliminate distractions from the environment, especially when you are doing anything new for the first time. So when you begin your encyclopedic knowledge Program, be especially careful to choose a quiet and non-chaotic time to introduce your *Bit of Intelligence* cards.

FREQUENCY

Space your Encyclopedic Knowledge sessions during the day so you are truly doing many brief sessions rather than sessions back to back, which are, in reality, long sessions. Intersperse them with reading sessions. After you have completed a session go to something else.

If your child cries "more" (as very often he will) say, "Of course, as soon as we have set the table!" Your child will be a glutton for all this. You must be the one who sees to it he never overdoes it, by always stopping after one session and always keeping your promise to bring out the *Bit of Intelligence* cards again later.

The morning hours are best to teach. Afternoon is generally not as good a time, but in the evening things start to pick up again. In any event, choose those times when your child is bright and alert, and avoid like the plague any time he is not.

INTENSITY

You have taken great care to insure that your

Bit of Intelligence cards are clear, big, and mounted with a good border around them. This guarantees that your child can see the subject of the cards very easily, and you can show your *Bit of Intelligence* cards quickly without worrying whether your child can see them or not.

Position yourself approximately eighteen inches from your child. Your hands must not obstruct the image of the card in any way.

The lighting should be good and you should eliminate visual, auditory and tactile distractions.

Another aspect is the intensity of your voice. The younger your child is when you begin, the louder and clearer your voice should be. Just don't shout.

DURATION

You should take one second and no longer per *Bit of Intelligence* card. You should always, always, always show your child a few cards less than he would really like you to show. If you know your child would love to see fifteen, you show ten; if ten is the maximum your child wants, show five.

Your child's attention is superb—make sure you always earn it by very brief, zippy, highly organized and enthusiastic sessions.

ONE DAY'S SESSIONS

Begin by introducing three different categories with ten *Bit of Intelligence* cards in each. Make sure you teach each category three times before the day ends. As your confidence grows, begin adding more categories day by day until you are doing ten different categories. Again each category is done for ten seconds three times daily.

ADDING NEW INFORMATION; RETIRING THE OLD

Ten days after you have reached ten categories, begin to retire one old *Bit of Intelligence* card from each category daily. Place these retired cards in your file for use later. Add one new *Bit of Intelligence* card to each category daily to replace the one you have retired. From this time on you continue to add one new card per category daily or a total of ten new *Bit of Intelligence* cards daily. *This is a minimum number not a maximum.*

If you can introduce new cards faster, there is no question but that your child can retain them. The minimum given here is a reflection of time spent searching, cutting and gluing. It is not a reflection of the capacity of the brain of a tiny child. For all intents and purposes that is without limit.

When you have run out of *Bit of Intelligence*

cards in a category, retire that category altogether and introduce a whole new category of ten cards in its place. Later when you have found enough new *Bit of Intelligence* material in the retired category you can reintroduce it. Meanwhile file the retired cards carefully, because you will be needing them later.

THE LIFE-SPAN OF ONE *BIT OF INTELLIGENCE* CARD

Every mother should be on top of her child's program. For example, she should know exactly how many times she needs to show her child a new *Bit of Intelligence* card before it becomes old hat to him. It is vital to know this because it should be changing all the time.

For instance, in the program outlined above, how many times does your child see a card before it is retired? If you have followed carefully, you will see that the life cycle of one *Bit of Intelligence* card is thirty sessions, because a new card is seen three times daily for ten days. However, if you do this program with energy and enthusiasm for three to six months, you will discover that thirty exposures over a ten day period is simply more than is necessary for your child.

Why is this?

You have been effective in growing the visual pathway of your child. Now you can show him his new cards only three times daily for five days (a total of fifteen times) and *voilá*—he knows them!

This tremendous change in frequency is commonly achieved within a few months of beginning the above program.

Once you begin, ask yourself often, "Do I need to change the life-cycle of the *Bit of Intelligence* cards in recognition of the increased maturity of my child's visual pathway?"

If you are enjoying yourself and your child is too, there is little doubt you will one day realize that your child needs to see new cards only once or twice to know them well.

Sometimes mothers see this as a problem. Then they realize they have achieved their objective—a child who can learn anything quickly and effortlessly the first time around. Your child's brain is growing every day and it is growing very quickly.

WHAT IS A "PROGRAM OF INTELLIGENCE"?

Once you have established a broad network of *Bit of Intelligence* cards, systematically arranged in categories, it is time to expand your Encyclopedic Knowledge Program.

When you have taught your child 1,000 *Bit of Intelligence* cards, you should start creating Programs of Intelligence.

While a category of intelligence establishes breadth of knowledge in an area, Programs of Intelligence provide an ascending magnitude of knowledge within a category. Each new program within a category adds a higher magnitude, starting with the most simple information and ending with the most profound. Here is an example:

Division: *Biology*
Category: *Birds*
***Bit of Intelligence* card:** *Common Crow*

1ST MAGNITUDE PROGRAM: *Crows build nests in trees or bushes.*

2ND MAGNITUDE PROGRAM: *Crows' nests are made of twigs lined with grass or hair.*

3RD MAGNITUDE PROGRAM: *Crows eat insects, seeds, fruit and nuts.*

4TH MAGNITUDE PROGRAM: *Crows have been known to eat mollusks, dead animals, mice, eggs, fish, garbage, rubber, putty and plastic insulation.*

5TH MAGNITUDE PROGRAM: *The female crow raises one brood per year.*

6TH MAGNITUDE PROGRAM: *The voice of the crow is harsh and loud, not musical.*

7TH MAGNITUDE PROGRAM: *Crows are part of the Corvidae Family.*

8TH MAGNITUDE PROGRAM: *The Corvidae Family is made up of Crows, Jays and Magpies.*

9TH MAGNITUDE PROGRAM: *Most birds of the Corvidae Family mate for life.*

10TH MAGNITUDE PROGRAM: *Most Corvidae are gregarious—they nest in dense colonies.*

11TH MAGNITUDE PROGRAM: *The only places in the world where there are not members of the Corvidae Family are New Zealand and most of the islands of the Pacific Ocean.*

12TH MAGNITUDE PROGRAM: *The Corvidae Family has 103 species in 26 different genera.*

Clearly these magnitudes go on and on and are limited only by the present state of human knowledge in any one area.

When you begin Programs of Intelligence your objective should be to establish breadth of knowledge across all of your categories, rather than continuing to increase the degree of magnitude of any single *Bit of Intelligence* card or category.

Initially you should aim to do a Program of Intelligence of the 1st Magnitude on every retired card in all your categories. As you complete this step you begin to build to higher and higher magnitudes in all of the categories.

As this is accomplished at ascending magnitudes, information about individual items within a category begins to overlap. Then categories themselves become interrelated.

In the end your Encyclopedic Knowledge Program becomes a vast network of knowledge in which no new piece of information is added without shedding light on some other piece of information.

When you have reached this stage you will find the more you teach your child, the more he will be able to hold.

This is a very nice state of affairs for him and for you.

OTHER CHARACTERISTICS OF PROGRAMS OF INTELLIGENCE

1. A Program of Intelligence is accurate.

It is a fact, not an opinion or an assumption. For example, "George Washington was the first president of the United States" is a Program of

Intelligence. "Zachary Taylor was a bad president" is not a Program of Intelligence—it's an opinion.

2. A Program of Intelligence is clear.

It is worded as clearly and directly as possible so it is not open to misinterpretation of any kind. For example, "The cheetah is the fastest mammal on earth" is a clear statement that cannot be misinterpreted.

Programs of Intelligence may be used to relate one retired category of *Bit of Intelligence* cards to another retired category.

For example, "George Washington was born in Virginia". For the child who knows George Washington and the state of Virginia, this is a nice neat way of tying two seemingly unrelated categories together.

As you and your child discover more ways to relate one category to another, your excitement in discovering the next new relationship will be greatly intensified. Programs of Intelligence should relate to information with which your child is already familiar.

It is quite true that Bach was called the Master of the fugue, but as a first program about Bach it is probably too esoteric.

"Bach had twenty-three children" will get you where you want to go better and faster. You can easily come back and give Programs of

Intelligence of greater magnitude about a man who had twenty-three children.

In short, you want initial Programs of Intelligence to open doors for your child. In order for your child to want to peek behind those doors, the initial programs need to relate to those things that he already knows. You may then cover quite unfamiliar ground without any difficulty.

Programs of Intelligence should be interesting. It is a fact that Philadelphia is "x" square miles but this is dry stuff unless you are doing mathematical programs and are headed somewhere with square miles. How much more interesting to know that Philadelphia is the home of the Liberty Bell.

If a fact you have found looks dry and dull to you, the chances are good it will look dry and dull to your child. Go for the things that excite your interest, and you will get your child's interest.

Programs of Intelligence should be amusing where it is appropriate. Humor is the most undervalued, underrated, underestimated teaching device which exists.

Few Programs of Intelligence made a bigger hit with the Institutes' kids than, "Tchaikovsky held his chin with his left hand while he conducted with his right hand because he was afraid his head would fall off."

The world is full of amazing and amusing facts—use them.

How to Find Programs of Intelligence

The first place to gather information about a retired *Bit of Intelligence* card is the source where you found the item in the first place. Some wise parents photocopy information found along with their drawings or photographs before mounting them and file that information. You will also need either a full encyclopedia or a good one-volume encyclopedia. If you can't afford to buy one, spend time at your local library.

A good junior high school dictionary and eventually a good college dictionary are also helpful to every aspect of your program. Such dictionaries should have word pronunciation guides and word derivations along with the definitions.

When in doubt look it up.

Don't give your child what you *think* is the truth. Check your facts as accurately as you possibly can.

How to Prepare Programs of Intelligence

There are three basic ways to present Programs of Intelligence. The easiest is to write the programs you are planning to teach on 5" x 7" index cards. Put five programs on each card. (You will be reading them to your child.)

```
                    Common Crow
1. Crows build nests in trees and bushes.
2. Crows' nests are made of twigs lined
   with grass or hair.
3. Crows eat insects, seeds, fruit and
   nuts.
4. Crows have been known to eat mollusks,
   dead animals, mice, eggs, fish garbage,
   rubber, putty and plastic insulation.
5. The female crow raises one brood per
   year.
```

Another way of teaching a program is to write it out on sentence cards in large print. You will also be reading it to him, but he will be able to see the words as you read them out.

This may become an important part of his reading program.

Crows eat insects, seeds, fruit and nuts.

Yet another way to introduce programs is to make a very nice homemade reading book with one program per page, five to ten programs per book. This is read by you to your child and later by your child to himself. Of course the size of print used is based on your child's reading level at that moment.

How to Teach Programs of Intelligence

ONE SESSION

One session should consist of no more than five programs. Programs take longer to read aloud than *Bit of Intelligence* cards and in order to keep sessions you need to do fewer of them.

If you are simply telling your child the programs, use an index card system to keep you straight. It is fun to dig out the five old *Bit of Intelligence* cards and show them quickly as you give your child some new information.

For example, you pull retired cards of birds and say as you show :

Crow–
"Crows build nests in trees or bushes."

Robin–
"Robins have red breasts and gray wings."

Bluejay–
"The call of the bluejay is 'jay' or 'jeeah.'"

Mockingbird–
"The mockingbird often sings at night."

Cardinal Grosbeak–
"The male cardinal grosbeak is bright red with a black mask."

This should take about 10–15 seconds. If you prefer to use large-print sentences instead of showing the actual *Bit of Intelligence* card, show the sentence as you read it.

If you prefer the book, sit down and read it with your child. Whichever way you decide to use it should be fast and a lot of fun.

ONE DAY'S SESSIONS

Begin with five categories of five programs each. Do each category three times in the day. You can expand this to include as many categories as you wish.

Adding New Programs and Retiring Old Ones

After five days retire all the programs you have been using and put in five new programs in each category. This means a new program will be done three times over five days, to total fifteen times before being retired. You will be adding at least twenty-five new programs every five days. If you see your child is learning his programs more quickly, retire them sooner and introduce new ones.

When you run out of good programs in a particular category, retire the category and begin working on another retired category.

Magnitudes of Programs

When you have done many Programs of Intelligence of the First Magnitude you begin to teach programs of the Second Magnitude. Each magnitude requires a broader general knowledge than the one before it. Therefore your first programs will contain new information but in a familiar context. You will use familiar vocabulary in initial programs. As you advance, your use of vocabulary becomes more and more sophisticated.

In this way your child is always reaching above his head for new information while at the same time standing on a firm foundation of understanding. It is up to you to make each step upward a combination of new information clothed in a context he can readily understand and appreciate.

Indeed the correct balance of these two elements is the foundation of all fine teaching.

Summary

By this point it should be clear to you that you can teach your child virtually anything that you can present in an honest and factual way. All the subjects that you know and love you can offer to your tiny child. All the subjects that you were interested in learning about but never had the opportunity to do you can now teach your child. Even those subjects with which you may have had difficulty now begin to be a possibility.

Indeed, mothers who have been teaching *Bit of Intelligence* cards to their children for twelve months or more find that their attitude toward knowledge and learning is completely changed. For such mothers the world is their oyster. There is no subject that is too formidable for them. They may not know every subject in the world, but they have a good idea of where to get any material they need for *Bit of Intelligence* cards. They have the world wired.

We are continually amazed at the endless imagination of our professional mothers and fathers. It is safe to say that no two mothers ever do exactly the same Encyclopedic Knowledge Program.

Each child's program is a unique reflection of the creativity, imagination and inventiveness of his mother. Like the ability of the tiny child, the inventiveness of a professional mother appears to be limitless.

Every mother who embarks upon this adventure expects to expand her tiny child's ability. She does this with such vim and vigor that she hardly takes the time to assess the changes that are taking place in her own abilities and viewpoint.

One day when she finds herself happily preparing to teach her child calculus or nuclear physics she is brought up short by her own bravado.

She is startled, but not for long.

"I always secretly knew I could learn anything," she says to herself and gets back to work teaching her child.

We are no longer able to learn at a good fraction of the speed of a tiny child, nor is the quality of our learning even comparable to his.

However, we have the thrill and the honor of taking this superb learner and gently lifting him onto our shoulders. What broad shoulders our professional parents have and what a panoramic view they provide for our tiny kids.

19

how is it possible
for infants to do
instant math?

The question is not "How is it possible for infants to do instant math?" but rather, "How is it possible for adults who speak a language not to do instant math?"

The problem is that in math we have mixed up the symbol, 5, with the fact,

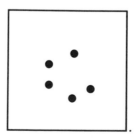

When the problem is on the order of 5 or

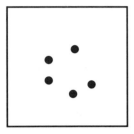

it is no problem since the adult can perceive
the symbol or the fact successfully from one

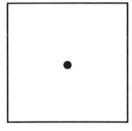

up to about 12

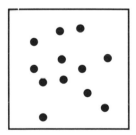

with some degree of reliability.

From 12

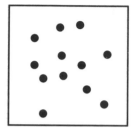

to about 20

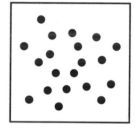

the reliability of even the most perceptive adult tends to descend sharply.

From 20

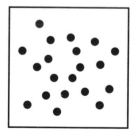

upward one is guessing and almost invariably guessing very badly indeed.

Children who already know symbols, for example 5, 7, 10, 13, but who do not know the facts

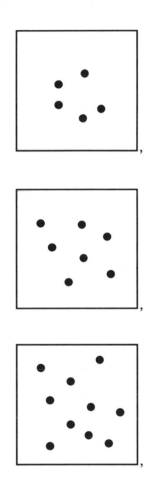

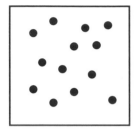

are unable to do instant math.

Tiny children, however, see things precisely as they are, while we adults tend to see things as we believe them to be or as we believe that they should be.

I find it maddening that, while I completely understand how children of two years can do instant math, I am unable to do the same. The reason I fail to do instant math is that if you say "seventy-nine" to me I am able to see only

I am not able to see

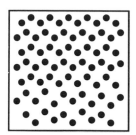

It is not precisely true to say that I cannot see the above. I can see it but I cannot perceive it.

Tiny children can.

In order for tiny children to perceive the truth of one (1) which is actually

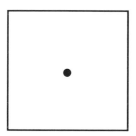

we need only show the child the fact

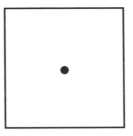

and say, "This is called one."
    We next present him with the fact

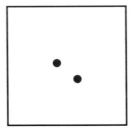

and say, "This is two."
    Next we say, "This is three," showing the child

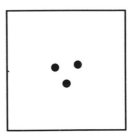

and so on. We need to present each of these a

very small number of times until the infant is able to perceive and retain the truth.

The adult mind, when faced with the fact, is inclined to astonishment, and many adults would rather believe that a child who is able to recognize

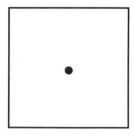

to

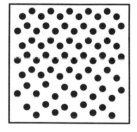

is in some way psychic than believe that a two-year-old can perform a task which we consider to be intellectual in nature and which we grown-ups cannot perform.

The next straw at which we grasp is the belief that the child is not truly recognizing the number but rather the pattern in which the numbers occur.

Any one-year-old worth his salt who has not been sucked into recognizing symbols before he recognizes the facts, can tell at a cursory glance that

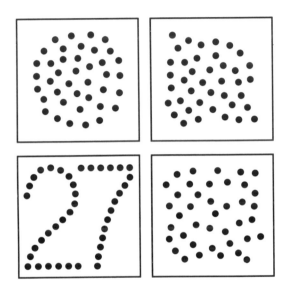

or whatever other way you choose to arrange the facts are all what we call—27? Sorry, we fooled you—in fact it's forty, not 27!

Which we grown-ups can see only if you present us with the symbol "40."

The kids are not fooled regardless of the form in which you present it and see only the truth, while we adults will actually have to count it up if you present it in any random pattern or to multiply it if you present it in an orderly columnar way. Thus if we present the fact in this form

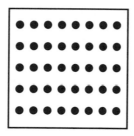

we solve the problem by actually counting, while the tiny child sees the truth at a glance.

If we present the truth in columnar form

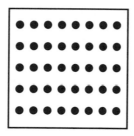

adults are inclined to count the number of rows across which we see as 8, and the number down, which we see as 5, and then to use an arithmetic form which we see as

$$
\begin{array}{r}
8 \\
\times\ 5 \\
\hline
40
\end{array}
$$

or an algebraic form: 8×5 = 40.

This incredibly slow process has almost nothing to recommend it except that it ultimately comes to a correct conclusion. However, even when it comes to the correct conclusion, which we see as 40, we have no idea what 40 actually means except by comparison with something else, such as the number of dollars I earn in a day, or a month plus ten days. The child sees the absolute truth which is that

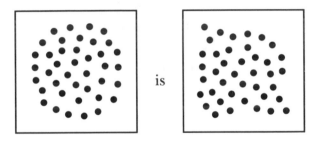

No more or less and no less.

If we must have the comparison with a month then it is fair to say that any child who has been given the chance to see the truth knows that

September, April, June and November have

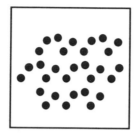

days.

And that if you must compare what we call 40 with a month then what we are talking about is

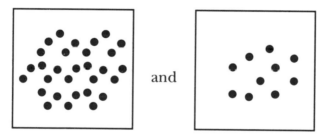

and

as any child can plainly see.

20

how to teach
your baby math

"Nina, how many dots can you see?"
"Why all of them, grandmother."

—Three-year-old Nina Pinkett Reilly

There are two vitally important reasons why tiny children should do mathematics. The first is the obvious and less important reason: Doing mathematics is one of the highest functions of the human brain—of all creatures on earth, only people can do math.

Doing math is one of the most important functions of life, since daily it is vital to civilized human living. From childhood to old age we are concerned with math. The child in school is faced with mathematical problems every day, as are the housewife, the carpenter, the business-man and the space scientist.

The second reason is even more important. Children should learn to do math at the youngest possible age because of the effect it will have on the physical growth of the brain it-self and the product of that physical growth —what we call intelligence.

Bear in mind that when we use the word *nu-meral* we mean the symbol that represents the *quantity* or true value, such as 1, 5, or 9. When we use the word *number* we mean the actual quantity of objects themselves, such as one, five, or nine:

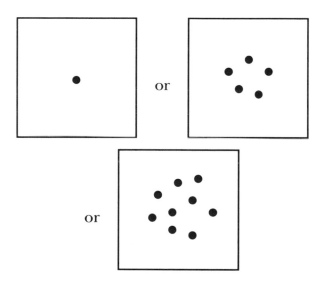

It is in this difference between true value or quantity and its symbolic representation by the use of symbols to represent actual quantity that tiny children find their advantage over adults.

You can teach your baby to do mathematics even if you aren't very good at doing it yourself. If you play the game of learning mathematics correctly both you and your child will enjoy it immensely. It takes less than a half-hour a day.

This chapter will give the basics of how to teach your baby mathematics. Parents who wish to have more information about the principles of teaching their babies math are advised to read the book *How to Teach Your Baby Math*.

Material Preparation

The materials used in teaching your child mathematics are extremely simple. They are designed in recognition that mathematics is a *brain* function. They recognize the virtues and limitations of the tiny child's visual apparatus and are designed to meet all of his needs from visual crudeness to visual sophistication and from brain function to brain learning.

All math cards should be made on fairly stiff white poster board so that they will stand up to frequent use.

In order to begin you will need:

1. A good supply of white poster board cut into 11" by 11" square cards. If possible, purchase these already cut to the size you want. This will save you a lot of cutting, which is much more time consuming than the remainder of the material preparation. You will need at least one hundred of these to make your initial set of materials.

2. You will also need 5,050 self adhesive red dots, 3/4" in diameter, to make cards 1 to 100. The Dennison Company makes *PRES-a-ply* labeling dots which are perfect for this purpose.

3. A large, red, felt-tipped marker. Get the widest tip available—the fatter the marker the better.

You will notice that the materials begin with large red dots. They are red simply because red is attractive to the small child. They are so designed in order that the baby's visual pathway, which is initially immature, can distinguish them readily and without effort. Indeed, the very act of seeing them will in itself speed the development of his visual pathway so that when we eventually teach numerals he will be able to see these numerals and learn them more easily than he otherwise would have.

You will begin by making the cards that you will use to teach your child quantity or the true value of numbers. To do this you will make a set of cards containing the red dots, from a card with one red dot to a card with one hundred red dots. This is time consuming but it is not difficult. There are, however, a few helpful hints that will make your life easier when you are making these materials:

1. Start with the one hundred card and work *backwards* down to one. The higher numbers are harder and you will be more careful at the start than at the finish.
2. Count out the precise number of dots *before* applying them to the card. (You'll have trouble in counting them after you have put them on the card especially when doing cards above twenty.)
3. Write the numeral in pencil or pen on all four corners of the back of the card *before* you place the correct number of dots on the front of the card.
4. Be sure *not* to place dots in a pattern such as a square, circle, triangle, or diamond or a shape of any other sort.

5. Place dots on the cards in a totally random way working outward from the middle, making certain that they do not overlap or touch each other.

6. Be careful to leave a little margin around the edges of your cards. This will provide a little space for your fingers to curl around the card and insure that you are not covering a dot with your fingers when you show the cards.

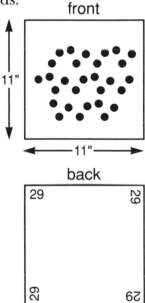

front

11"

◄——11"——►

back

29   29

29   29

Making the above materials does take some time and depending on the cost of the poster board can be somewhat expensive, but compared to the thrill and excitement you and your child will have doing math together it should be worth your effort.

There is a kit now available from the Better Baby Press with these cards already made up for parents.

These first one hundred cards are all you need to begin step one of your math program.

Once you begin to teach your child mathematics you will find that your child goes through new material very quickly.

We discovered a long time ago that it is best to start out ahead. For this reason, make all one hundred dot cards before you actually begin to teach your child. Then you will have an adequate supply of new material on hand and ready to use. If you do not do this, you will find yourself constantly behind.

Remember—the one mistake a child will not tolerate is to be shown the same material over and over again long after it should have been retired.

Be smart—start ahead in material preparation and stay ahead. And if for some reason you do get behind in preparing new materials, do not fill in the gap by showing the same old cards again. Stop your program for a day or a week until you have reorganized and made new material, then begin again where you left off.

Start out ahead and stay ahead.

THE MATH PATHWAY

The path that you will now follow in order to teach your child is amazingly simple and easy. Whether you are beginning with an infant or an eighteen-month-old the path is essentially the same.

The steps of that path are as follows:

First Step	Quantity Recognition
Second Step	Equations
Third Step	Problem Solving
Fourth Step	Numeral Recognition
Fifth Step	Equations with numerals

THE FIRST STEP (*Quantity Recognition*)

Your first step is teaching your child to be able to perceive actual numbers, which are the true value of numerals. Numerals, remember, are merely symbols to represent the true value of numbers. You will begin by teaching your baby (at the youngest age possible down to birth) the dot cards from one to ten. You will begin with cards one to five.

Begin at a time of day when your child is receptive, rested and in a good mood.

Use a part of the house with as few distracting

factors as possible, in both an auditory and a visual sense; for instance, do *not* have the radio playing and avoid other sources of noise. Use a corner of a room that does not have a great deal of furniture, pictures, or other objects that might distract your child visually.

Now the fun begins. Simply hold up the "one" card just beyond his reach and say to him clearly and enthusiastically, "This is one." Show it to him very briefly, no longer than it takes to say it. One second or less.

Give your child no more description. There is no need to elaborate.

Next, hold up the "two" card and again with great enthusiasm say, "This is two."

Show the three, four, and five card in precisely the same way as you have the first two cards. It is best when showing a set of cards to take the card from the back of the set rather than feeding from the front card. This allows you to glance at one of the corners of the back of the card where you have written the number. This means that as you actually say the number to your child you can put your full attention on his face. You want to have your full attention and enthusiasm directed toward him rather than looking at the card as he looks at it.

Remember, the more quickly you show him the cards, the better his attention and interest will be. Remember also that your child will have had your happy and undivided attention and there is nothing that a tiny child loves more than that.

Do not ask your child to repeat the numbers as you go along. After the five card has been shown give your child a huge hug and kiss and display your affection in the most obvious ways. Tell him how wonderful and bright he is and how much you love teaching him.

Repeat this two more times during the first day, in exactly the manner described above. In the first few weeks of your math program, sessions should be at least one half-hour apart. After that, sessions can be fifteen minutes apart.

The first day is now over and you have taken the first step in teaching your child to understand mathematics. (You have thus far invested at most three minutes.)

The second day, repeat the basic session three times. Add a second set of five new dot cards (six, seven, eight, nine and ten). This new set should be seen three times throughout the day. Since you now will be showing two sets of five cards, and each set will be taught three times in the day, you will be doing a total of six math sessions daily.

The first time you teach the set of cards from

one to five and the set of cards from six to ten you may show them in order (i.e., one, two, three, four, five.) After that *make sure that you always shuffle each set of cards before the next showing so that the sequence in which your child will see the cards is unpredictable.*

Just as with reading, at the end of each session tell your child he is very good and very bright. Tell him that you are very proud of him and that you love him very much. Hug him and express your love for him physically, don't bribe him or reward him with cookies, candy, or the like.

Again, as with reading, children learn at lightning speed—if you show them the math cards more than three times a day you will bore them. If you show your child a single card for more than a second you will lose him. Try an experiment with his dad. Ask Dad to stare at a card with six dots on it for thirty seconds. You'll find that he'll have great difficulty in doing so. Remember that babies perceive much faster than grown-ups.

Now you are teaching your child two sets of math cards with five cards in each set, each set three times a day. You and your child are now enjoying a total of six math sessions spread out during the day, equaling a few minutes in all.

Remember: the only warning sign in the entire

process of learning math is boredom. *Never bore the child. Going too slowly is much more likely to bore him than going too quickly.*

Consider the splendid thing you have just accomplished. You have given your child the opportunity to learn the true quantity of ten when he is actually young enough to perceive it. This is an opportunity you and I never had. He has done, with your help, two most extraordinary things.

1. His visual pathway has grown and, more important, he is able to differentiate between one quantity or value and another.

2. He has mastered something that we adults are unable to do and, in all likelihood, never will do.

Continue to show the two sets of five cards but after the second day mix the two sets up so that one set might be three, ten, eight, two and five while the remaining cards would be in the other set. This constant mixing and reshuffling will help to keep each session exciting and new. Your child will never know which number is going to come up next. This is a very important part of keeping your teaching fresh and interesting.

Continue to teach these two sets of five cards in this way for five days. On the sixth day you will begin to add new cards and put away old cards.

Here is the method you should use from this point on in adding new cards and taking out old ones. Simply remove the two lowest numbers from the ten cards you have been teaching for five days. In this case you would remove the one card and the two card and replace those cards with two new cards (eleven and twelve.) From this point on you should add two new cards daily and put away two old cards. We call this process of putting away an old card "retirement." However, every retired card will later be called back to active duty when we get to the second and third steps, as you will see shortly.

DAILY PROGRAM
(after the first day)

Daily Content:	2 sets
One Session:	1 set (5 cards) shown once
Frequency:	3 x daily each set
Intensity:	3/4-inch red dots
Duration:	5 seconds per session
New Cards:	2 daily (1 in each set)
Retired Cards:	2 daily (two lowest)
Life Span of Each Card:	3 x daily for 5 days = 15 x

Principle: Always stop before your
child wants to stop.

In summary, you will be teaching ten cards daily, divided into two sets of five cards each. Your child will be seeing two new cards daily or one new card for each set and the two lowest cards will be retired each day.

Children who have already been taught to count from one to ten or higher may attempt to count each card at first. Knowing how to count causes minor confusion to the child. He will be gently discouraged from doing this by the speed at which the cards are shown. Once he realizes how quickly the cards are shown, he will see that this is a different game from the counting games he is used to playing and should begin to learn to recognize the quantities of dots that he is seeing. For this reason, if your tiny child does not know how to count, do not introduce it until *well after* he has completed steps one through five of this pathway.

Again, one must remember the supreme rule of never boring the child. If he is bored there is a strong likelihood that you are going too slowly. He should be learning quickly and pushing you to play the game some more.

If you have done it well he will be averaging two new cards daily. This is actually a *minimum* number of new cards to introduce daily. You may feel that he needs new material more quickly. In this case, you should retire three cards daily and add three new ones or even four.

By now both parent and child should be approaching the math game with great pleasure and anticipation. Remember, you are building into your child a love of learning that will multiply throughout his life. More accurately, you are reinforcing a built-in rage for learning that will not be denied but which can certainly be twisted into useless or even negative channels in a child. Play the game with joy and enthusiasm. You have spent no more than three minutes teaching him and five or six loving him and he has made one of the most important discoveries he will ever make in his whole life.

Indeed, if you have given him this knowledge eagerly and joyously and as a pure gift with no demands of repayment on the child's part, he will have already learned what few adults in history have ever learned. He will actually be able to *perceive* what you can only *see*. He will actually be able to distinguish thirty-nine dots from thirty-eight dots or ninety-one dots from ninety-two dots. He now knows *true* value and not merely symbols and has the basis he needs to truly understand math and not merely memorize formulas and rituals such as "I put down the 6 and carry the 9." He will now be able to recognize at a glance forty-seven dots, forty-seven pennies, or forty-seven sheep.

If you have been able to resist testing, he may now have demonstrated his ability by accident. In either case, trust him a bit longer. Don't be misled into believing he can't do math this way merely because you've never met an adult who could. Neither could any of them learn English as fast as every kid does.

You continue to teach the dot cards, in the way described here, all the way up to one hundred. It is not necessary to go beyond one hundred with the quantity cards, although a few zealous parents have done so over the years. After one hundred you are only playing with zeros. Once your child has seen the dot cards from one to one hundred he will have a very fine idea of quantity.

In fact, he will need and want to begin on the second step of the Math Pathway well *before* you get all the way up to one hundred in the dots. When you have completed one to twenty with the dot cards, it is time to begin the second step.

THE SECOND STEP (*Equations*)

By this time your child will have quantity recognition from one to twenty. At this point there is sometimes the temptation to review old cards over and over again. Resist this temptation. Your child will find this boring. Children love to learn new numbers but they do not love to go over and over old ones. You may also be tempted to test your child. Again, do not do this. Testing invariably introduces tension into the situation on the part of the parent and children perceive this readily. They are likely to associate tension and unpleasantness with learning. We have discussed testing in greater detail earlier in the book.

Be sure to show your child how much you love and respect him at every opportunity.

Math sessions should always be a time of laughter and physical affection. They become the perfect reward for you and your child.

Once a child has acquired a basic recognition of quantity from one to twenty, he is ready to begin to put some of these quantities together to see what other quantities result. He is ready to begin addition.

Beginning to teach addition equations is very easy. In fact, your child has already been watching the process for several weeks.

Every time you showed him a new dot card, he saw the addition of one new dot. This becomes so predictable to the tiny child that he begins to anticipate cards he has not yet seen. However, he has no way of predicting or deducing *the name* we have given the condition of "twenty-one." He has probably deduced that the new card we are going to show him is going to look exactly like twenty except it is going to have *one more dot on it.*

This of course is called addition. He doesn't know what it is called yet but he does have a rudimentary idea about what it is and how it works. It is important to understand that he will have reached this point *before* you actually begin to show him addition equations for the first time.

You can prepare your materials by simply writing two-step addition equations on the backs of your cards in pencil or pen. A few moments with your calculator and you can put quite a number on the back of each dot card from one to twenty. For example the back of your ten card should look like this:

9 + 1 = 10	5 + 5 = 10
8 + 2 = 10	2×5 = 10
7 + 3 = 10	5×2 = 10
6 + 4 = 10	1 + 2 + 3 + 4 = 10
20÷2 = 10	19 − 9 = 10
30÷3 = 10	18 − 8 = 10
40÷4 = 10	17 − 7 = 10
50÷5 = 10	16 − 6 = 10

To begin, place on your lap face down the one, two and three cards. Using a happy and enthusiastic tone simply say "One plus two equals three." As you say this you show the card for the number you are saying.

Therefore for this particular equation you hold up the one card and say "one" (put down the one card) and say "plus" (pick up the two card) and say "two" (put down the two card) and say "equals" (pick up the three card) and say " three."

He learns what the word "plus" and the word

"equals" mean in the same way he learns what the words "mine" and "yours" mean, which is by seeing them in action and in context.

Do this quickly and naturally. Again practice on Dad a few times until you feel comfortable. The trick here is to have the equation set up and ready to go before you draw your child's attention to the fact that a math session is about to begin. It is foolish to expect your baby to sit and watch you shuffle around for the correct card to make the equation that you are about to show him. He will simply creep away, and he should. His time is valuable too.

Set up the sequence of your equation cards for next day *the night before* so that when a good time presents itself you are ready to go. Remember, you will not be staying on the simple equations of one to twenty for long; soon you will be doing equations that you cannot do in your head so readily or so accurately.

Each equation takes only a few seconds to show. Don't try to explain what "plus" or "equals" means. It is not necessary because you are doing something far better than explaining what they mean, you are demonstrating what they are. Your child is seeing the process rather than merely hearing about it. Showing the equation defines clearly what "plus" means and what "equals" means. This is teaching at its best.

If someone says, "One plus two equals three" to an adult, what he sees in his mind's eye is 1 + 2 = 3, because we adults are limited to seeing the symbols rather than the fact.

What the child is seeing is

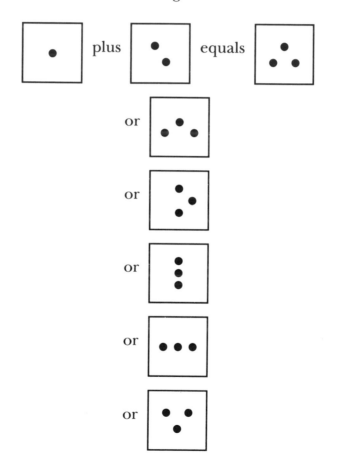

Tiny children see the fact and not the symbol.

Always be consistent about the way you say the equations. Use the same words each time. Say, "One plus two equals three." Don't say, "One and two makes three." When you teach children the facts, they will deduce the rules, but we adults must be consistent for them to deduce the rules. If we change the vocabulary we use, children have a right to believe that the rules have changed also.

Each session should consist of three equations—no more. You may do less than this but do not do more. Remember you always want to keep the sessions brief.

Do three equation sessions daily. Each of these three sessions will contain three different equations; therefore, you will be doing *nine different equations daily.* Please note you do not have to repeat the same equation over and over again. Each day your equations will be new.

Please avoid doing predictable patterns of equations in one session. For example

$$1 + 2 = 3$$
$$1 + 3 = 4$$
$$1 + 5 = 6$$

etc.

A much better session would be

```
1 + 2 =  3
2 + 5 =  7
4 + 8 = 12
```

Keep the addition equations to two steps because this keeps the session zippy and crisp, which is much better for the tiny child.

One hundred and ninety different two-step addition equations that can be made using the cards between one and twenty, so don't be afraid that you will run out of ideas in the first week. You have more than enough material here to work with.

In fact, after two weeks of nine addition equations daily, it is time to move on to subtraction or you will lose the attention and interest of your child. He has a clear idea about adding dots; now he is ready to see them subtracted.

The process you will use to teach subtraction is exactly the same as the process you have used to teach addition. This is the same method by which he learns English.

Prepare your dot cards by writing various equations on the back. Begin by saying, "Three minus two equals one." Again you will have the three cards that make up each equation on

your lap and you will show each card as you say
the number

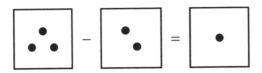

By now you will have gone beyond twenty in
teaching the dot cards so you will have an even
wider selection of numbers to use to make subtraction equations and you should feel free to
use these higher numbers as well.

Now you can stop doing addition equations
and replace these sessions with subtraction
equations. You will be doing three subtraction
equation sessions daily with three different
equations in each session while you are simultaneously continuing two sets of five dot cards
three times daily in order to teach the higher
numbers up to one hundred. This gives you
nine very brief math sessions in a day.

DAILY PROGRAM

Session 1	Dot Cards
Session 2	Subtraction Equations
Session 3	Dot Cards
Session 4	Dot Cards

Session 5	Subtraction Equations
Session 6	Dot Cards
Session 7	Dot Cards
Session 8	Subtraction Equations
Session 9	Dot Cards

Each of these equations has the great virtue that the child knows both quantities

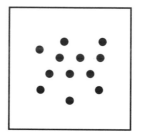

and their names (twelve) beforehand. The equation contains two elements that are satisfying to the child. First, he enjoys seeing old dot cards he already knows and second, although he already knows these two quantities, he now sees that his two old quantities subtracted create a new idea. This is exciting to him. It opens the door for understanding the magic of mathematics.

During the next two weeks you will be majoring in subtraction. During this time you will show approximately 126 subtraction equations to your child. That is plenty. You do not have to do every possible combination. Now it is time to move on to multiplication.

Multiplication is nothing more than repeated addition, so it will not come as any great revelation to your child when you show him his first multiplication equation. He will, however, be learning more of the language of mathematics and this will be very helpful to him.

Since your child's repertoire of dot cards has been growing daily you now have even higher numbers that you can use in your multiplication equations. Not a moment too soon, because you will need higher numbers now to supply answers to these equations. Prepare your cards by writing as many multiplication equations as possible on the back of each dot card.

Using three cards say, "Two multiplied by three equals six ."

He will learn what the word "multiplied" means in exactly the same way that he learned what the words "plus," "equals," "minus," "mine," and "yours" mean, by seeing them in action.

Now your subtraction equation sessions will be replaced by multiplication equation sessions. You will do three sessions daily with three equations in each session. Follow exactly the same pattern you have been following with addition and subtraction. Meanwhile continue the dot card sessions with higher and higher numbers.

Under ideal circumstances your tiny child has seen only *real numbers* in the form of dot cards and has not, as yet, seen any numeral, not even 1 or 2.

The next two weeks are devoted to multiplication. Continue to avoid predictable patterns in the equations that you do in one session, such as

$$
\begin{aligned}
2\times3 &= 6 \\
2\times4 &= 8 \\
2\times5 &= 10
\end{aligned}
$$

These patterns do have a value later in the book. We will touch upon when to bring them to the attention of your child, but not just yet. For the moment we want to keep the tiny child wondering what is coming next. The question, "What's next ?" is the hallmark of the tiny child and each session should provide him with a new and different solution to that mystery.

You and your child have been enjoying math

together for less than two months and you have already covered quantity recognition from one to one hundred, addition, subtraction, and multiplication. Not bad for the small investment of time required to do so and the excitement and adventure of learning the language of mathematics.

We have said that you have now completed all the dot cards, but this is not quite true. There is actually one quantity card left to teach. We have saved it until last because it is a special one and particularly beloved of tiny children.

It has been said that it took ancient mathematicians five thousand years to invent the idea of zero. Whether that is the case or not, it may not surprise you to learn that once tiny children discover the idea of quantity they immediately see the need for no quantity.

Little children adore zero and our adventure through the world of real quantity would not be complete without including a zero dot card. This one is very easy to prepare. It is simply an 11" by 11" piece of white poster board with no dots on it.

The zero dot card will be a hit every time. You will now use the zero card to show your child addition, subtraction and multiplication equations. For example:

Now we have, in fact, completed teaching all the real number cards that we need. However, we are not finished with the dot cards. We will still be using them in many ways to introduce new mathematical ideas as we go along.

After two weeks of multiplication it is time to move on to division. Since your child has completed all the dot cards from zero to one hundred, you may use all these cards as the basis for your division equations. Prepare your cards by writing two-step division equations on the backs of many, if not all, of your one hundred dot cards. (This is a great job for the resident mathematician. If you don't happen to have one, try using Dad.)

Now you simply say to your child, "Six divided by two equals three ."

He will learn what the word "divided" means exactly as he learned what every other word means. Each session contains three equations. You do three sessions daily so you will cover nine division equations daily. By now this will be very easy indeed for you and your child.

When you have spent two weeks on division equations, you will have fully completed the second step and will be ready to begin the third step on the pathway.

THE THIRD STEP (*Problem-Solving*)

If up to now you have been extraordinarily giving and completely non-demanding, then you are doing very well and you haven't done any testing.

We have said much about teaching and much about testing.

Our strongest advice on this subject is do *not* test your child. Babies love to learn, but they hate to be tested. In that way they are very like grown-ups.

Well what is a mother to do? She does not want to test her child; she wants to teach him and give him every opportunity to experience the joy of learning and accomplishment.

Therefore, instead of testing her child she provides problem-solving opportunities.

The purpose of a problem-solving opportunity is for the child to be able to demonstrate what he knows if he wishes to do so.

It is exactly the *opposite* of the test.

Now you are ready not to *test* him but to *teach* him that he knows how to solve problems (and you'll learn that he can.)

A very simple problem-solving opportunity would be to hold up two dot cards. Let's say you choose "fifteen" and "thirty-two" and you hold them up and ask, "Where is thirty-two?"

This is a good opportunity for a baby to look at or touch the card if he wishes to do so. If your baby looks at the card with thirty-two dots on it or touches it, you are naturally delighted and make a great fuss. If he looks at the other card simply say, "This is thirty-two, isn't it?" while holding up the thirty-two card in front of him.

You're happy, enthusiastic, and relaxed. If he does not respond to your question, hold the card with thirty-two dots a little closer to him and say, "This is thirty-two, isn't it?" again in a happy, enthusiastic, relaxed way.

End of opportunity.

No matter how he responds, he wins and so do you, because the chances are good that if you are happy and relaxed he will enjoy doing this with you.

These problem-solving opportunities can be put at the end of equation sessions. This creates a nice balance of give and take to the session, since each session begins with you giving three equations to your child and ends with an opportunity for your child to solve one equation if he wishes to do so.

You will find that merely giving your child an opportunity to choose one number from another is all right to begin with, but you should very shortly move on to opportunities to choose answers to equations. This is a lot more exciting for your child, not to mention for you.

To present these problem-solving opportunities you need the same three cards you would need to show any equation, plus a fourth card to use as a choice card. *Don't ask your child to say answers. Always give him a choice of two possible answers.* Very young children do not speak or are just beginning to speak. Problem-solving situations which demand an oral response will be very difficult if not impossible for them. Even children who are beginning to speak do not like to answer orally (which is in itself another test) so always give your child a choice of answers.

Remember that you are not trying to teach your child to talk, you are teaching him mathematics. He will find choosing to be very easy and a lot of fun, but he will quickly become irritated if we demand speech.

Since you have now completed all the dot cards and addition, subtraction, multiplication, and division at the initial stages, you can make your equation sessions even more sophisticated and varied. Continue to do three equation sessions daily. Continue to show three completely different equations at each session. But now it is unnecessary to show all three cards in the equation. Now you need only show the answer card.

This will make the sessions even faster and easier. You simply say, "Twenty-two divided by eleven equals two" and show the "two" card as you say the answer. It is as simple as that.

Your child already knows "twenty-two" and "eleven" so there is no real need to keep showing him the whole equation. Strictly speaking there is no real need to show him the answer either, but we have found that it is helpful for us adults to use visual aids when we teach. The kids seem to prefer it also.

Now the equation sessions will be composed of a variety of equations, for example an addition equation, a subtraction equation, and a division equation.

Now would also be a good time to move on to three-step equations and see if your child enjoys them. If you move quickly enough through the material the chances are very good that he will.

Simply sit down with a calculator and create one or two three-step equations for each card and write them clearly on the back of each one. A typical session at this point would be

Equations:

$$2\times2\times3 = 12$$
$$2\times2\times6 = 24$$
$$2\times2\times8 = 32$$

Problem-Solving:

$$2\times2\times12 = \ ?$$

48 or 52

Please note that these sessions continue to be very, very brief. Your child now has nine three-step equations daily with one problem-solving opportunity tagged onto each session.

Therefore you are giving him the answer to the first three equations in each session and, at the end of each session, giving him the opportunity to choose the answer to the fourth equation if he wishes to do so.

After a few weeks of these equations, it is time to add a little additional spice to your sessions again. Now you are going to give your child the type of equations which he will like best of all.

Begin to create equations which combine two of the four functions of addition, subtraction, multiplication, and division.

Combining two functions gives you an opportunity to explore patterns by creating equations that are related by a common element. For example:

$$3 \times 15 + 5 = 50$$
$$3 \times 15 - 5 = 40$$
$$3 \times 15 \div 5 = 9$$

or

$$40+15-30 = 25$$
$$40+15-20 = 35$$
$$40+15-10 = 45$$

or

$$100-50\div10 = 5$$
$$50-30\div10 = 2$$
$$20-10\div10 = 1$$

Your child will find these patterns and relationships interesting and important—just as all mathematicians do.

When you are creating these equations, it is important to remember if you are using multiplication in the equation that the multiplication function must come first in the sequence of the equation. Otherwise you can feel free to make up any equations that you wish as long as the ultimate answer to the equation falls between zero and one hundred since you do not have any dot cards beyond one hundred. Write these new equations on the back of each dot card.

Your problem-solving opportunities should contain these more advanced equations as well.

After a few weeks time add another function

to the equations you are offering. Now you will be giving four-step equations for the first time, for example:

$$56+20-16\div2 = 30$$
$$56+20-8\div2 = 34$$
$$56+20-4\div2 = 36$$

These four-step equations are a great deal of fun. If you were a little intimidated at first by the idea of teaching your child mathematics, by now you should be relaxing and really enjoying these more advanced equations just as your child is enjoying them.

From time to time you should feel free to show three unrelated equations as well as those which have a pattern. For example:

$$86+14-25\div5 = 15$$
$$100\div25+0-3 = 1$$
$$3\times27\div9+11-15 = 5$$

It is true that he will actually be perceiving what is happening, while you and I can only see the equations without truly digesting the information. Nevertheless there is no small pleasure in the knowledge that you and you alone have brought about this ability in your child.

You will be astonished at the speed at which your child solves equations. You will wonder if he solves them in some psychic way. When adults see two-year-olds solving math problems faster than adults can, they make the following assumptions in the following order:

1. The child is guessing. (The mathematical odds against this, if he is virtually always right, are astronomical.)

2. The child isn't actually perceiving the dots but instead is actually recognizing the pattern in which they occur. (Nonsense. He'll recognize the number of men standing in a group, and who can keep people in a pattern? Besides, why can't you recognize the seventy-five pattern on the seventy-five dot card which he knows at a glance?)

3. It's some sort of trick. (You taught him. Did you use any tricks?)

4. The baby is psychic. (Sorry but he isn't: he's just a whiz at learning facts. We'd rather write a book called "How to Make Your Baby Psychic" because that would be

even better. Unfortunately we don't know how to make little kids psychic.)

Now the sky is the limit. You can go in many directions with mathematical problem-solving at this point and the chances are extremely good that your child will be more than willing to follow you wherever you decide to go.

For those mothers who would like some further inspiration we include some additional ideas

1. Sequences
2. Greater than and less than
3. Equalities and inequalities
4. Number personality
5. Fractions
6. Simple algebra

It is not possible to cover all of these areas within the scope of this book. However, these areas are covered in more detail in the book *How To Teach Your Baby Math.*

All of these can be taught using the dot cards and indeed should be taught using the dot cards because in this way the child will see the reality of what is happening to real quantities rather than learning how to manipulate symbols as we adults were taught.

THE FOURTH STEP (*Numerals*)

This step is ridiculously easy. We can now begin the process of teaching the numerals or symbols that represent the true values or quantities that your child already knows so well.

You will need to make a set of numeral cards for your child. It is best to make a complete set from zero to one hundred. These should be on 11" by 11" poster board and the numerals should be made with the large, red, felt-tipped marker. Again, you want to make the numerals very large—6" tall and at least 3" wide. Make sure to make your strokes wide so that the numerals are in bold figures.

Be consistent about how you print. Your child needs the visual information to be consistent and reliable. This helps him enormously.

Always label your materials on the upper left-hand side. If you do this you will always know that you have them right side up when you are showing them to your child.

This is not a consideration with the dot cards you have already made to show quantity since there is no right-side-up or upside down to those cards. In fact, you want to show those cards every which way they come up—that is why on the back of the dot cards you have labeled all four corners, not just the upper left-hand corner.

On the back of the numeral cards, print the numeral again in the upper left-hand corner. Make this whatever size is easy for you to see and read. You may use pencil or pen to do this.

Your numeral cards should look like this:

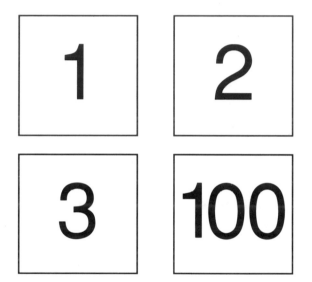

Sometimes mothers get fancy and use stencils to make their cards. This makes beautiful numeral cards; however, the time involved is prohibitive. Remember that your time is precious.

Neatness and legibility are far more important than perfection. Often mothers find that fathers can make very nice cards and that they appreciate having a hand in the math program.

At this stage in your daily program you are

doing three sessions a day of equations with a bit of problem-solving at the end of each of those sessions, but you have long since finished the six sessions you used to do in order to teach the dot cards initially. Now you will teach the numeral cards in exactly the same way that you taught the dot cards several months ago.

You will have two sets of numeral cards with five cards in each set. Begin with 1 to 5 and 6 to 10. You may show them in order the first time but after that always shuffle the cards so that the sequence is unpredictable. As before, each day retire the two lowest numerals and add the next two. Make sure that each set being shown has a new card in it every day rather than one set having two new cards and the other set remaining the same as the day before.

Show each of the sets three times daily. Please note that your child may learn these cards incredibly quickly, so be prepared to go even faster if necessary. If you find that you are losing your child's attention and interest, speed up the introduction of new material. Instead of retiring two cards daily, retire three or four cards and put in three or four new cards. At this point you may find that three times daily is too high a frequency. If your child is interested during the first two sessions each day but consistently creeps away for the third session, then drop the frequency from three times daily to two times daily.

You must at all times be sensitive to your child's attention, interest, and enthusiasm. These elements when carefully observed will be invaluable tools in shaping and reshaping your child's daily program to suit his needs as he changes and develops.

At the very most it should take you no longer than fifty days to complete all the numerals from zero to one hundred. In all likelihood it will take a lot less time.

Once you have reached the numeral one hundred you should feel free to show a variety of numerals higher than one hunded. Your child will be thrilled to see numerals for 200, 300, 400, 500, and 1,000. After this come back and show him examples of 210, 325, 450, 586, 1,830. Don't feel that you must show each and every numeral under the sun. This would bore your child tremendously. You have already taught him the basics of numeral recognition by doing zero to one hundred. Now be adventurous and give him a taste of a wide diet of numerals.

When you have taught the numerals from zero to twenty it is time to begin a bridging step of relating the symbols to the dots. There are a multitude of ways of doing this. One of the easiest ways is to go back to equalities, inequalities, greater than, and less than and use dot cards and symbol cards together.

Take the dot card for 10 and put it on the floor, then put down the not equal sign, then the numeral card 35 and say, "Ten is not equal to thirty-five."

One session would look like this:

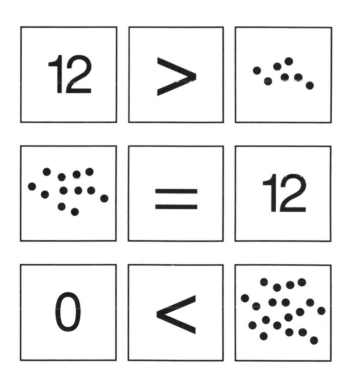

As you work your way up through the numeral cards, play this game with as many numeral cards and dots cards as you have the time and inclination to do. Children also like to join in and choose their own combinations using the dot cards and the numeral cards.

Learning the numerals is a very simple step for your child. Do it quickly and joyously so you can get on to the fifth step as soon as possible.

THE FIFTH STEP (*Equations with numerals*)

The fifth step is really a repetition of all that has come before. It recapitulates the entire process of addition, subtraction, multiplication, division, sequences, equalities, inequalities, greater than, less than, square roots, fractions, and simple algebra.

Now you will need a good supply of poster board cut into strips 18" long and 4" wide. These cards will be used to make equation cards using numerals. At this stage we recommend that you switch from using red to black felt-tipped marker. The numerals you will be writing now will be smaller than before and black has greater contrast than red for these smaller figures. Your numerals should be 2" tall and 1" wide.

Your first cards would look like this:

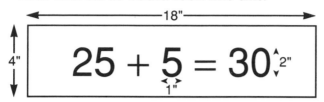

Now go back to Step Two of the pathway and follow the instructions, only this time use new equation cards with numerals instead of the dot cards. When you have completed Step Two go on to Step Three.

For Step Three you will need to make some materials suitable for problem-solving opportunities. Now make a quantity of cards to use which do not have answers written on them. Again use single numeral cards to provide your child with choice cards. It will be helpful if you always write the correct answer on the top left hand corner of these problem-solving cards along with the problem itself so that you are never at a loss to know what the answer really is.

$$25 + 5$$

25 + 5 = 30

(reverse)

Here are some examples of what your materials will look like as you work your way through the operations that you have already done with dots.

Subtraction Equations

$$30 - 12 = 18$$

$$92 - 2 - 10 = 80$$

$$100 - 23 - 70 \neq 0$$

Multiplication Equations

$$3 \times 5 = 15$$

$$14 \times 2 \times 3 = 84$$

$$15 \times 3 \times 2 \times 5 \neq 45$$

Division Equations

$$76 \div 38 = 2$$

$$192 \div 6 \div 8 = 4$$

$$84 \div 28 = 3$$

$$458 \div 2 = 229$$

Continue to use these 2" size numerals long enough to be sure that your child is comfortable with them. When this part of your program is going smoothly, you can begin making the numerals smaller. This must be a gradual process. If you make your numerals too small too quickly you will lose the attention and interest of your child.

When you have gradually reduced the numeral size to one inch or smaller, you will have more space on the cards to write longer and more sophisticated equations. As part of your problem-solving program at this point your child may wish to choose numerals and operational symbols (=, ≠, +, −, ×, ÷) and make his own equations for you to answer. Keep your calculator handy—you will be needing it!

Summary

When you have completed the first through the fifth steps of the Math Pathway you will have reached the end of the beginning of your child's life-long adventure in mathematics. He will have had a superbly joyous introduction into the world of arithmetic. He will have mastered four basic but vital truths in mathematics.

First, he will have learned about quantity. Indeed he will be able to differentiate many different quantities from one another.

Second, he will have learned how to put those quantities together and take those quantities apart. He will have seen hundreds of different combinations and permutations of quantities.

Third, he will have learned that there are symbols that we use to represent the reality of each of the quantities and how to read those symbols.

And finally and most important, he will know the difference between the reality of quantity and the symbols that have arbitrarily been chosen to represent those quantities.

Arithmetic will be the end of the beginning for him because he will now easily and happily be able to make the leap from the simple mechanics of arithmetic to the much more fascinating and creative world of higher mathematics. This is a world of thinking and reasoning and logic: not merely predictable calculations but instead a genuine adventure where new things are discovered all the time.

Sadly, this is a world that very few have ever entered. The majority of us escaped from mathematics at the earliest possible moment and long before the exciting world of higher mathematics was in view. Indeed it has always been considered a closed shop where only a lucky few gain entrance. Instead of arithmetic being a springboard to higher mathematics, it closed the doors to this wonderful language.

Every child should have the right to master this superb language. You will have bought your child his passport.

21

the magic is
in the child
... and in you

There are only two lasting bequests
we can give our children.
One is roots , the other wings.

—HODDING CARTER

The most important part of how to multiply
your baby's intelligence is learning what your
baby really is and what he has the potential to
become.

You now have learned the basic details of how
to teach your baby as well. But beware— we
human beings treasure techniques. We love
"know-how." In fact, we Americans pride ourselves on our know-how. But sometimes we place
know-how before "know why" in importance. We
should not do so.

The principles of how the brain grows and why it grows the way it does are infinitely more important than the techniques or the how-to's.

There is no magic in the techniques.

The magic is in the child.

Do not fall in love with techniques.

Instead be certain you have gained a thorough understanding of how the brain grows and why it grows in the way that it does.

It is infinitely more important.

If you learn *only* techniques, no matter how well you learn them you will lack the certainty and confidence that understanding the principles and philosophy give you. Under these circumstances you will carry out the techniques poorly.

As time goes by and you begin to forget the techniques, your knowledge will degenerate and you will know less and less.

On the other hand, if you truly understand what you are doing and why you're doing it, your knowledge will grow by leaps and bounds and in the end you will be able to invent more techniques and even better techniques than we have taught you in this book.

We have spent years developing these techniques and they are splendid. What is most important, they work and work well. But there is one thing you must never forget:

The magic is not in the techniques, the magic is in the child. The magic is in his incredible brain. The magic is in you.

A staff member was once flying from Sydney to San Francisco. It's a long trip. Sitting beside him was a young mother, brimming over with enthusiasm about a recent adventure. He listened delightedly while she told him about a marvelous course she had taken in Philadelphia called "How to Multiply Your Baby's Intelligence."

When she wound down a bit, he asked her, "And do these things work?"

"Yes, of course they work," she replied.

"So you have actually begun to teach your daughter to read—and to do math and all of those things."

"Yes, a little," she responded, "and it's fun. But that is not really the most important thing."

"Oh, then what is?" he asked.

"Why, our whole lives are changed and they will be forever."

"Really?"

"Of course they are. I've always loved her dearly and now I love her even more because now I respect her more and understand her much better. I fully understand the magnitude of the miracle in a way that I never did before.

"Now we love and respect each other more

than I would have believed possible. As a result, I talk to her and deal with her in an entirely different way than I ever would have done before. If I had never shown her a reading word or a single math card our lives would still have been totally changed by the experience."

That mother knew the magic was in her child.

We parents are the best thing that ever happened to babies, but we have, in the past half century, been bullied into doing some strange things.

We love our children very much and because we do we put up with all the dirty diapers, the runny noses, the momentary terror when for a second we lose sight of them on a crowded beach, the high temperatures which seem to happen only at 2:00 a.m., the flying trips to the hospital and all the rest that goes with the territory of being parents and loving our kids.

But when it comes time to introduce them to all of the breath-taking beauty that there is in the world—everything beautiful that has been written in our languages, all the gorgeous paintings that were ever painted, all the moving music that was ever written, all the wonderful sculptures that were ever carved—we wait until they are six years old, when it's just about over, and then tragically turn that joyful opportunity over to a stranger called a teacher who often doesn't think that it's a joyful opportunity.

We miss the magic that is born of mother and father and tiny baby learning together. The most magical learning team this world has ever seen.

We sometimes are bullied into doing some mighty strange things.

The magic of every child is born in him. It comes with him and if we are wise enough to recognize and nurture it, the magic stays with him the rest of his life. If we respect the magic we become part of it.

Every mother and father has experienced a sense of wonder and astonishment when gazing upon their own newborn baby.

Every parent knows that magic.

The magic is not in the cardboard and the red markers, it is not in the dots , and it is certainly not in the school system. The magic is not even in the Institutes for the Achievement of Human Potential.

The magic is in your child. He has his own unique brand of magic, unlike any magic that has ever been seen before.

Find that magic and give him yours.

If this book provides one mother with a new and profound respect for her baby, then it will have been well worth the effort. For this, all by itself, will bring about a powerful and important change for every mother and baby so touched.

This is what the Gentle Revolution is all about.

acknowledgments

If history records who wrote the first book, the information hasn't filtered down to me.

Whoever he or she was, I'm sure of one thing–it wasn't done without a good deal of help from other people.

The Good Lord knows that, while I've been working on this book for forty years in one way or another, I certainly had giant amounts of help, all of it vital.

In the most direct way, there have been Janet Doman, Michael Armentrout and Susan Aisen, who actually wrote several of the chapters in their entirety. Those chapters are so brilliantly clear and incisive that I am at once delighted that they are, while simultaneously a bit chagrined that the rest of the book is less so.

Lee Pattinson vetted it word for word and removed the splinters of my split infinitives. Lee's doing so lightened the burden of my long-time Doubleday editor and friend, Ferris Mack, whose "snide marginal notes" were witty and kind enough to render painless the removal of some of my favorite phrases regarding some of my favorite people in the whole world.

The hundreds of thousands of words which were in one or another of the several manuscripts were typed by Greta Erdtmann and Cathy Ruhling, who managed to act as if that endless tedium was actually enjoyable.

Michael Armentrout designed the book and, without a single complaint, put it together in various forms to suit my "whims of iron", which must have seemed endless.

That peerless Canadian artist and photographer Sherman Hines did all the photography, except where otherwise noted.

Old Hippocrates, Temple Fay and many other great neurosurgeons and neurophysiologists are there on every page, as are the great teachers I have had. (The dreadful teachers I have had are also there, albeit in a different way).

That group of people whom I can only describe as sublime, the Staff of the Institutes for the Achievement of Human Potential, are on every page, in every word and in the spaces in between. They range in age and experience from ninety-year-old Professor Raymond Dart, whose discovery of *Australopithecus Africannus Dartii* changed man's idea of who we are, and from whence we came–forever, to the tireless twenty-one-year-old aspirants.

So also, on every page, are the many thousands of superb children we have learned from, ranging as they do from the most severely brain-injured comatose child to the truly Renaissance Children of the Evan Thomas Institute.

To speak of those children and their individually unique accomplishments is to laud their endlessly determined and determinedly cheerful and heroic parents who live in a joyous world of their own design. To name one or a hundred or a thousand of them would somehow diminish the remaining thousands. I herewith salute them all–child, woman and man–and bow to them with the most profound love and respect.

I wish to acknowledge that largely unsung group, the Board of Directors of the Institutes, both living and dead, who have given us their love, devotion guidance and, upon more than one occasion, have risked their precious reputations to support us when we were attacking the status quo so jealously guarded by the self-appointed and self-anointed "sole proprietors of the truth".

Last, and far from least, I bow gratefully to all who have supported the work of the

Institutes down through all the years. They have given us their unwavering support in financial, emotional, intellectual, scientific and moral terms and in a thousand other ways.

about the authors

GLENN DOMAN received his degree in physical therapy from the University of Pennsylvania in 1940. From that point on, he began pioneering the field of child brain development. In 1955, he founded The Institutes for the Achievement of Human Potential in Philadelphia. By the early sixties, the world-renowned work of The Institutes with brain-injured children had led to vital discoveries about the growth and development of well children. The author has lived with, studied and worked with children in more than 100 nations, ranging from the most civilized to the most primitive. The Brazilian government knighted him for his outstanding work on behalf of the children of the world.

Glenn Doman is the international best-selling author of the Gentle Revolution Series, consisting of *How to Teach Your Baby to Read, How to Teach Your Baby Math, How to Multiply Your Baby's Intelligence, How to Give Your Baby Encyclopedic Knowledge*, and *How to Teach Your Baby to Be Physically Superb*. He is also the author of *What to Do About Your Brain-Injured Child*, a guide for parents of hurt children. Currently, he continues to devote all of his time teaching parents of both hurt and well children.

For more than thirty years Glenn Doman and the child brain developmentalists of The Institutes have been demonstrating that very young children are far more capable of learning than we ever imagined. He has taken this remarkable work—work that explores why children from birth to age six learn better and faster than older children do—and given it practical application. As the founder of The Institutes for the Achievement of Human Potential, he has created a comprehensive early development program that any parent can follow at home.

When Glenn Doman decided to update the books of the Gentle Revolution Series it was only natural that his daughter help him to edit and organize the additional information gained over the last three decades of experience since some of the books were originally written.

JANET DOMAN is the director of the Institutes for the Achievement of Human Potential. After completing studies in zoology at the University of Hull in England and physical anthropology at the University of Pennsylvania, she devoted herself to teaching early reading programs to parents at The Institutes. She spent almost two years at the Early Development Association in Japan where she created programs for mothers. From there she returned to Philadelphia to direct the Evan Thomas Institute, a unique school for mothers and babies. The early development program led to the creation of the International School for the children who graduated from the early development program.

Janet spends most of her day nose-to-nose with "the best mothers in the world," helping them to discover the vast potential of their babies and their own potential as teachers.

index

OTHER RELATED BOOKS, VIDEOS & KITS IN THE GENTLE REVOLUTION SERIES

HOW TO TEACH YOUR BABY TO READ

Glenn Doman and Janet Doman

How to Teach Your Baby to Read provides your child with the skills basic to academic success. It shows you just how easy and pleasurable it is to teach a young child to read. It explains how to begin and expand the reading program, how to make and organize your materials, and how to more fully develop your child's potential. *Paperback $9.95 / Hardback $18.95*

Also available: **How To Teach Your Baby To Read™ Video Tape**
How To Teach Your Baby To Read Kit

HOW TO TEACH YOUR BABY MATH

Glenn Doman and Janet Doman

How to Teach Your Baby Math instructs you in successfully developing your child's ability to think and reason. It shows you just how easy and pleasurable it is to teach a young child math. It explains how to begin and expand the math program, how to make and organize your materials, and how to more fully develop your child's potential. *Paperback $9.95 / Hardback $15.95*

Also available: **How To Teach Your Baby Math Video™ Tape**
How To Teach Your Baby Math Kit

HOW TO GIVE YOUR BABY ENCYCLOPEDIC KNOWLEDGE

Glenn Doman

How to Give Your Baby Encyclopedic Knowledge provides a program of visually stimulating information designed to help your child take advantage of his or her natural potential to learn anything. It shows you just how easy and pleasurable it is to teach a young child about the arts, science, and nature. Your child will recognize the insects in the garden, know the countries of the world, discover the beauty of a painting by Van Gogh, and more. It explains how to begin and expand your program, how to make and organize your materials, and how to more fully develop your child's mind. *Paperback $9.95 / Hardback $19.95*

Also available: **How To Give Your Baby Encyclopedic Knowledge™ Video Tape**
How To Give Your Baby Encyclopedic Knowledge Kit

HOW TO MULTIPLY YOUR BABY'S INTELLIGENCE

Glenn Doman and Janet Doman

How to Multiply Your Baby's Intelligence provides a comprehensive program that will enable your child to read, to do mathematics, and to learn about anything and everything. It shows you just how easy and pleasurable it is to teach your young child, and to help your child become more capable and confident. It explains how to begin and expand this remarkable program, how to make and organize your materials, and how to more fully develop your child's potential. *Paperback $12.95 / Hardback $24.95*

Also available: **How To Multipy Your Baby Intelligence™ Kit**

HOW TO TEACH YOUR BABY TO BE PHYSICALLY SUPERB

Glenn Doman, Douglas Doman and Bruce Hagy

How to Teach Your Baby to Be Physically Superb explains the basic principles, philosophy, and stages of mobility in easy-to-understand language. This inspiring book describes just how easy and pleasurable it is to teach a young child to be physically superb. It clearly shows you how to create an environment for each stage of mobility that will help your baby advance and develop more easily. It shows that the team of mother, father, and baby is the most important athletic team your child will ever be a part of. It explains how to begin, how to make your materials, and how to expand your program. This complete guide also includes full-color charts, photographs, illustrations, and detailed instructions to help you create your own program. *Hardback $24.95*

WHAT TO DO ABOUT
YOUR BRAIN-INJURED CHILD

Glenn Doman

In this breakthrough book, Glenn Doman—pioneer in the treatment of the brain-injured—brings real hope to thousands of children, many of whom are inoperable, and many of whom have been given up for lost and sentenced to a life of institutional confinement. Based upon the decades of successful work performed at The Institutes for the Achievement of Human Potential, the book explains why old theories and techniques fail, and why The Institutes philosophy and revolutionary treatment succeed. *Paperback $11.95 / Hardback $19.95*

CHILDREN'S BOOKS

About the Books

Very young readers have special needs. These are not met by conventional children's literature which is designed to be read by adults *to* little children not *by* them. The careful choice of vocabulary, sentence structure, printed size, and formatting is needed by very young readers. The design of these children's books is based upon more than a quarter of a century of search and discovery of what works best for very young readers.

ENOUGH, INIGO, ENOUGH

written by Janet Doman   illustrated by Michael Armentrout

Ages 1 to 6. *Hardcover $14.95*

NOSES IS NOT TOES

written by Glenn Doman   illustrated by Janet Doman

Ages 1 to 3. *Hardcover $14.95*

THE MOOSE BOOK

written by Janet Doman   illustrated by Michael Armentrout

Ages 2 to 6. *Paperback $9.95*

THE WRONG COCKATIEL

written by Michael Armentrout

Ages 3 to 6. *Paperback $9.95*

NANKI GOES TO NOVA SCOTIA

written by Michael Armentrout

Ages 3 to 6. Paperback $9.95

For a complete catalog of Avery books, call us at 1-800-548-5757.

COURSE OFFERINGS AT THE INSTITUTES

HOW TO MULTIPY YOUR BABY'S INTELLIGENCE™ COURSE

WHAT TO DO ABOUT YOUR BRAIN-INJURED CHILD COURSE

For more information regarding the above courses, call or write:

**The Institutes for the Achievement of Human Potential
8801 Stenton Avenue
Philadelphia, PA 19118 USA**

**1-800-344-MOTHER or 1-215-233-2050
or FAX 1-215-233-3940**